50 GEMS OF
East Kent

PAUL HARRIS

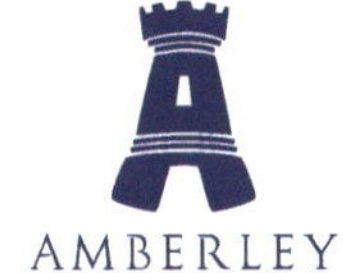

AMBERLEY

Acknowledgements

I would like to thank Owen Leyshon of Romney Marsh Countryside Partnership for advice on photographic restrictions at Dungeness; Candida Wright for her photographs of St Thomas à Becket's Church at Fairfield, the Romney, Hythe and Dymchurch Railway steam engine, her etching of the East Kent Downs and for laboriously helping me choose which images to use and which to leave out; Sarah Vickery kindly supplied the photograph of the inside of Margate's Shell Grotto and Steve Boulding the photograph of the Devil's Kneading Trough near Wye. All other photographs are by the author. Finally I would like to thank Judith Hemmings for typing up the manuscript and Philip and Pam Taylor whose generous help ensured this project reached its conclusion.

First published 2019

Amberley Publishing
The Hill, Stroud
Gloucestershire, GL5 4EP

www.amberley-books.com

Copyright © Paul Harris, 2019

Map contains Ordnance Survey data © Crown copyright and database right [2019]

The right of Paul Harris to be identified as the Author
of this work has been asserted in accordance with the
Copyrights, Designs and Patents Act 1988.

British Library Cataloguing in Publication Data.
A catalogue record for this book is available from the British Library.

ISBN 978 1 4456 7050 8 (print)
ISBN 978 1 4456 7051 5 (ebook)

Origination by Amberley Publishing.

Printed in Great Britain.

Appointed GPSR EU Representative: Easy Access System Europe Oü, 16879218

Address: Mustamäe tee 50, 10621, Tallinn, Estonia

Contact Details: gpsr.requests@easproject.com, +358 40 500 3575

Contents

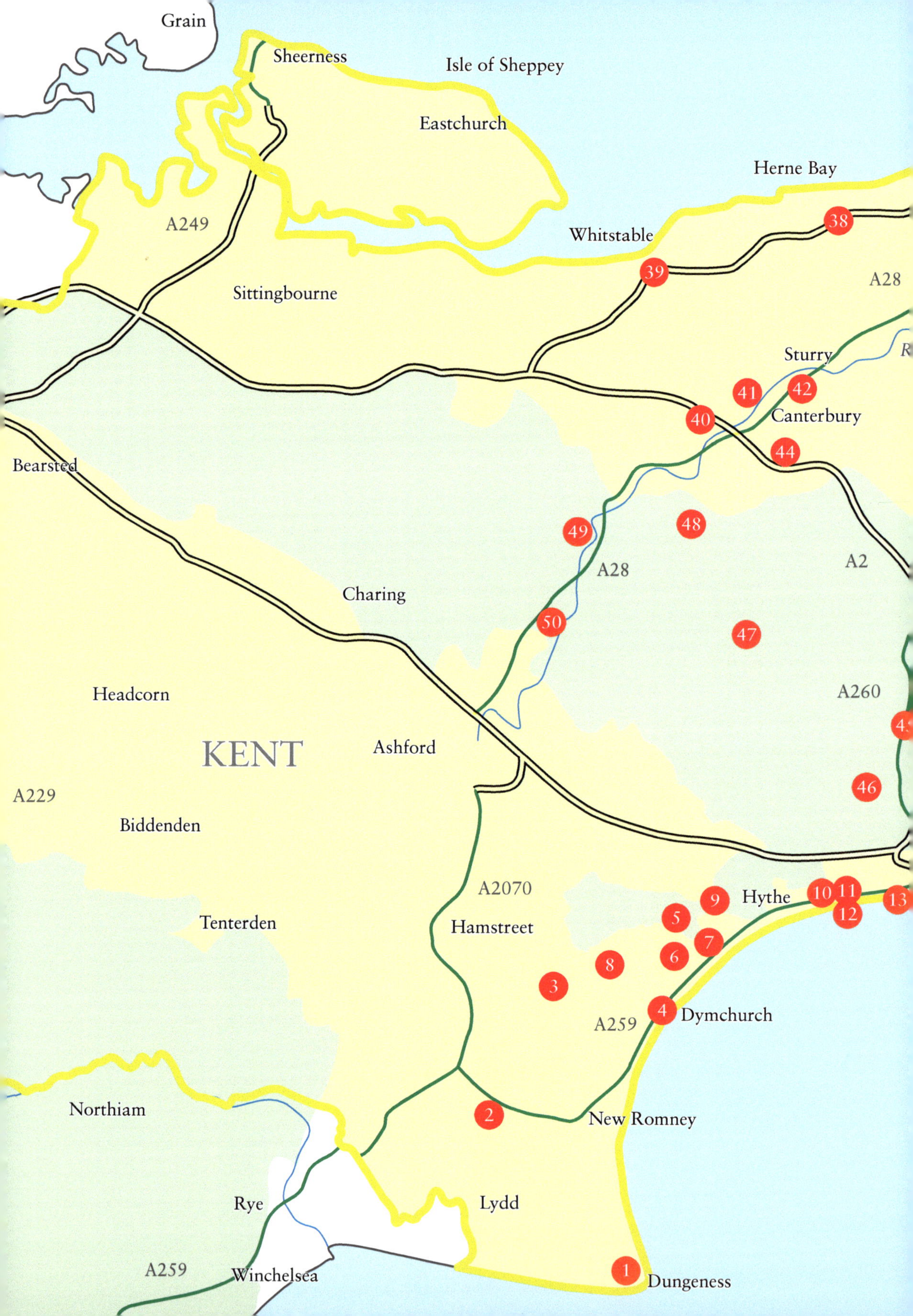

Grain
Sheerness
Isle of Sheppey
Eastchurch
Herne Bay
38
A249
Whitstable
39
A28
Sittingbourne
Sturry
R
41
42
40
Canterbury
44
Bearsted
49
48
A28
A2
Charing
50
47
A260
Headcorn
43
KENT
Ashford
A229
46
Biddenden
A2070
10 11
9
Hythe
13
Tenterden
5
Hamstreet
7
12
8
6
3
2
4 Dymchurch
A259
Northiam
2
New Romney
Rye
Lydd
A259
1
Winchelsea
Dungeness

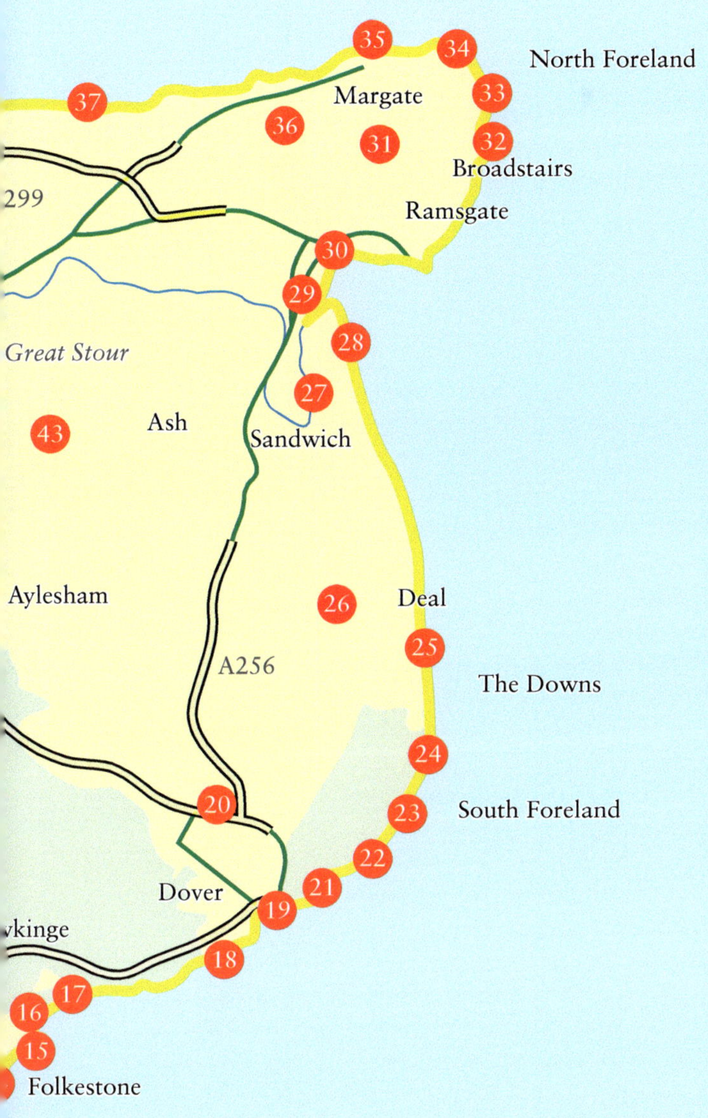

North Foreland
Margate
Broadstairs
Ramsgate
299
Great Stour
Ash
Sandwich
Aylesham
Deal
A256
The Downs
South Foreland
Dover
vkinge
Folkestone
STRAIT OF DOVER

Introduction

Kent, the 'Garden of England', is a large county stretching from the pleasant woods and villages of its western borders to the busy Channel coast, with its famous white cliffs and the long convoluted shorelines of the North Sea and Thames Estuary.

There is so much to visit, see and experience in Kent: magnificent castles, historic churches, hidden villages, dramatic coastline, pleasant resorts, rolling green downs and stunning views – it's all here. There is so much, in fact, that it was impossible to choose just fifty for one book, so I decided that East Kent deserved a volume to itself – not to mention it is the area where I grew up and have lived for most of my life. It is the area that I know and love and can speak most informatively about.

I have defined 'East Kent' as that part of the county that lies east of an imaginary line drawn from a point on the coastline in the north between Whitstable and Faversham, down past Ashford to the Kent–Sussex border on the Channel coast near the bleak shingle promontory of Dungeness.

Needing to restrict my choice of 'gems' to fifty has meant making choices in order to ensure that some of the more secret places and features are included, as well as the well-known attractions. My choices are personal ones and, in common with other titles in this series, I have not concerned myself too much with such things as transport connections, opening times, car parking, refreshment facilities and so on. Such information is notoriously changeable and is readily available online or via tourist information centres and leaflets. These pages are intended more as a stimulant to personal discovery than a fact file.

Starting in the open landscape of Romney Marsh, I move along the coastline of East Kent before turning inland towards the historic cathedral city of Canterbury and into the rural heart of this part of the county with its hidden valleys and villages, woodlands and downland views.

Hopefully this will be a book that appeals not only to the interested visitor but also to locals, who may discover in its pages more of the interest, richness and beauty to be found not far from home. So, without further ado, let us begin our journey. I hope you will enjoy it.

Romney Marsh and Hythe

1. Dungeness

I start in perhaps Kent's most desolate place: the strange, bleak expanse of Dungeness. This huge shingle promontory is said to be the largest such area in Europe and apparently qualifies as Britain's only desert landscape.

Artists, film makers, fashion shoots and naturalists (particularly birdwatchers) all love this place – for different reasons, of course. Most people, even casual visitors, find something fascinating in this large open landscape, hosting seemingly sparse vegetation and littered with numerous 'bits and bobs' – fishermen's huts, old boats, items like the strange net tanning boiler structure, capstans, wooden walkways and so on. This otherworldly feel is enhanced by the presence on the western side of Dungeness of two nuclear power stations (one now decommissioned) and a line of electricity pylons marching off to the empty horizon.

Appearances can be deceptive, though. This seemingly barren landscape hosts some 600 plant species (that is around half the total of UK species), a wide variety of insects (including the Sussex Emerald moth, which is only found in Britain at Dungeness), rare bumblebees and a thriving colony of the medicinal leech. A large part of Dungeness is designated a National Nature Reserve and 1,200 acres of that a Royal Society for the Protection of Birds (RSPB) reserve, which includes water-filled gravel pits used by many migratory birds. Notable among these are the very beautiful and unusual black, grey and white sinew. A colony of the rare common gull is also to be found here. These gravel pits are apparently the best place in Britain in which to find the earlier mentioned medicinal leech, so there is plenty to engage the interest of the naturalist here, but there is more.

The Romney, Hythe and Dymchurch Railway has its terminus at Dungeness and brings numerous visitors. These and the many coach parties arriving by road wander about the shingle expanse taking photographs, looking at the local

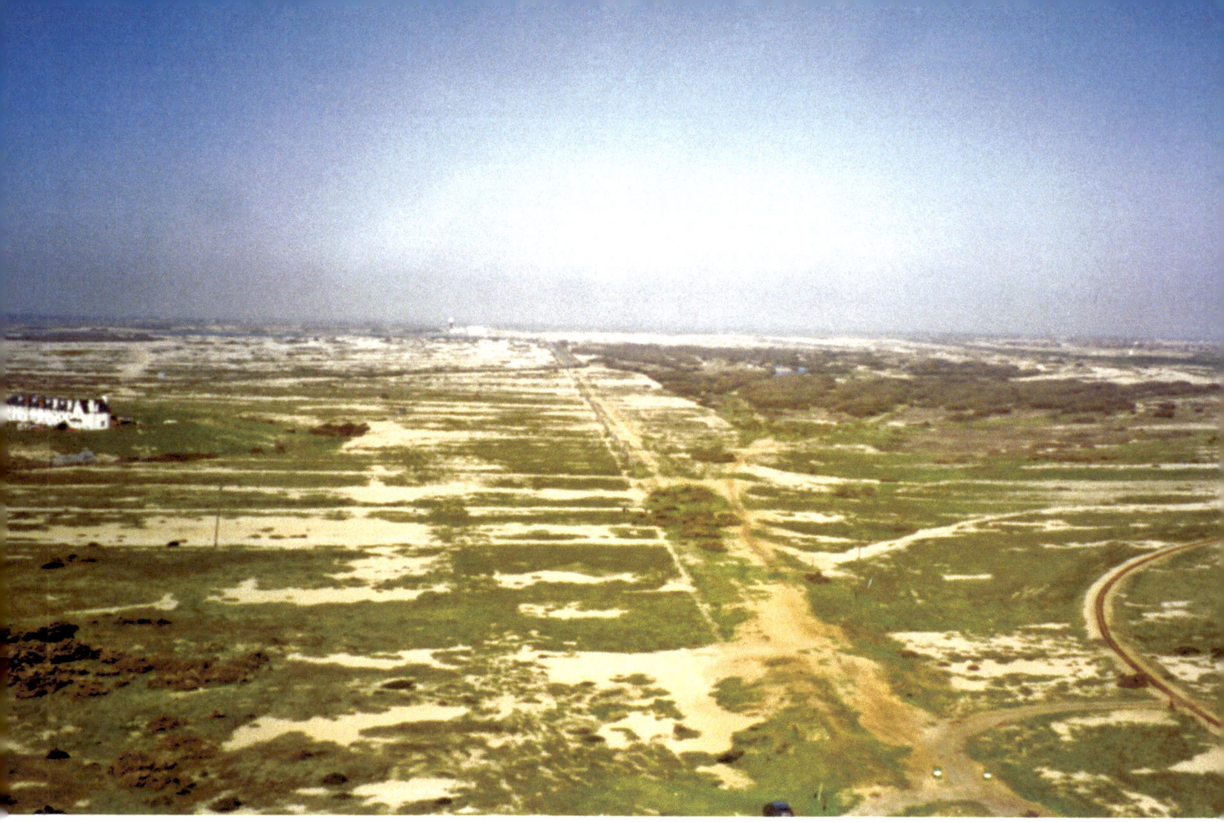

Above: The desolate landscape of Dungeness.

Below: 'Tan copper' and other bits and bobs in the Dungeness landscape.

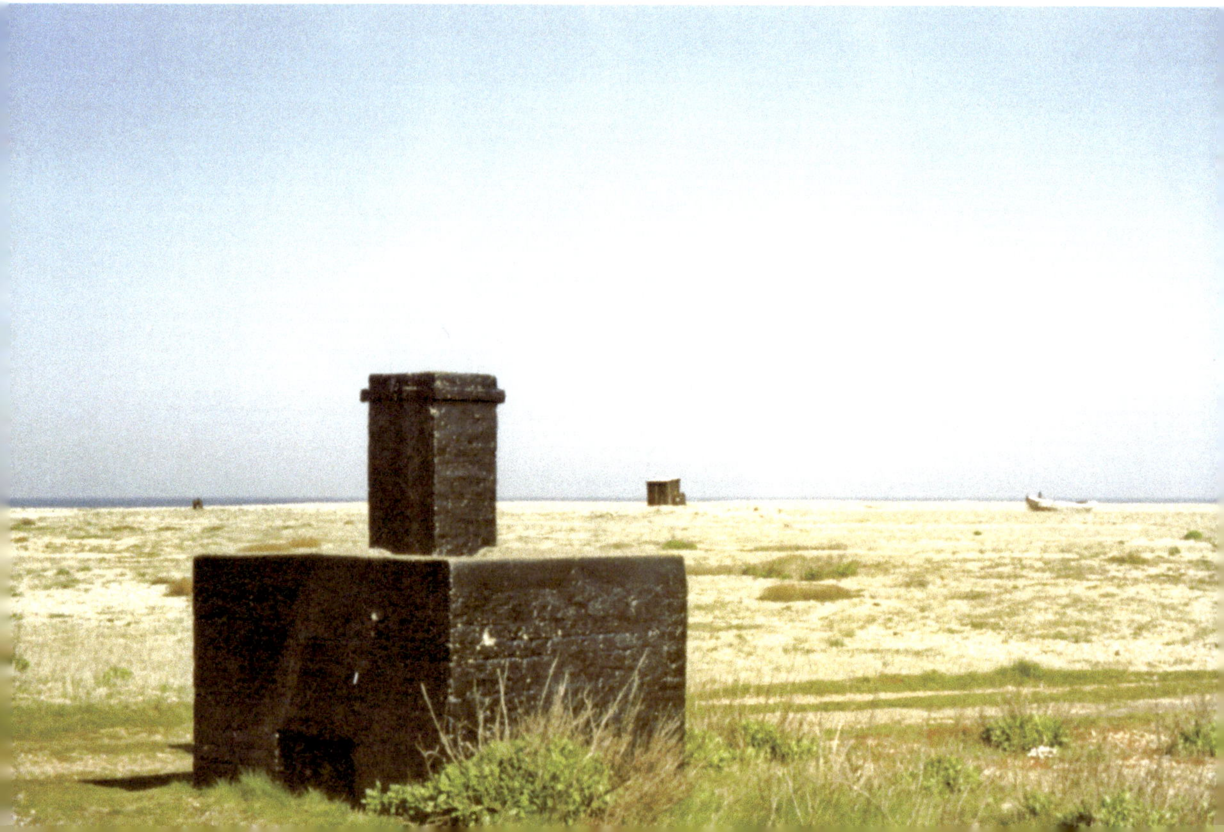

artworks, ascending the Old Lighthouse for spectacular views, buying smoked fish from a hut on the beach or enjoying the local fish (fried with chips) at popular pubs the Britannia and the Pilot Inn. Some 500,000 visitors a year come to Dungeness and unfortunately this can cause problems. The shingle environment, with its sea kale and sea pea, rare moths and birds, can be damaged by too many people leaving the paths and board walks and wandering about willy nilly. There is also the issue of residents' privacy. Many of the unusual shack-like buildings are private dwellings – the late Derek Jarman's cottage, for instance – so don't traipse all around them looking in the windows please. The respectful visitor, though, is of course always welcome.

2. St Thomas à Becket Church, Fairfield

There can be few more evocative sights on Romney Marsh than the lonely church of St Thomas à Becket at Fairfield. It sits on raised ground in low-lying pasture land surrounded by dykes and grazing sheep. There is no associated graveyard, and until 1913 the church could only be accessed by boat when the fields flooded during the winter months. The flooding still happens, of course, during wet years but access is now somewhat easier, using a causeway linking the road with the artificial mound upon which the church was built in around 1200. The church was dedicated to St Thomas Becket, who had been responsible during his lifetime for much drainage and land reclamation work in this vicinity.

The interior of the church is filled with box pews and has a triple-decker pulpit. The top level of this was used by the preacher to deliver the sermon, the middle stage was for the minister conducting the service and the lowest stage was for the parish clerk. The fine timber framing in the church is a good example of Georgian work. It is hard to imagine there ever being much of a congregation here such is the sparsity of dwellings in the vicinity, and there must have been times when winter access problems discouraged use of the church.

St Thomas à Becket's Church at Fairfield has been used to great effect as a setting for the 2011 BBC TV adaptation of the Charles Dickens's novel *Great Expectations* and in the 2012 feature film of the same name.

The church is kept locked but the key can be obtained from a nearby farm. Instructions for finding the key are posted on the door of the church and at the farm on the opposite side of the road.

Fairfield is one of a number of places on Romney Marsh that have interesting churches. You might also like to visit St Mary the Virgin Church at St Mary in the Marsh, St Augustine's at Brookland and St Nicholas Church at Old Romney.

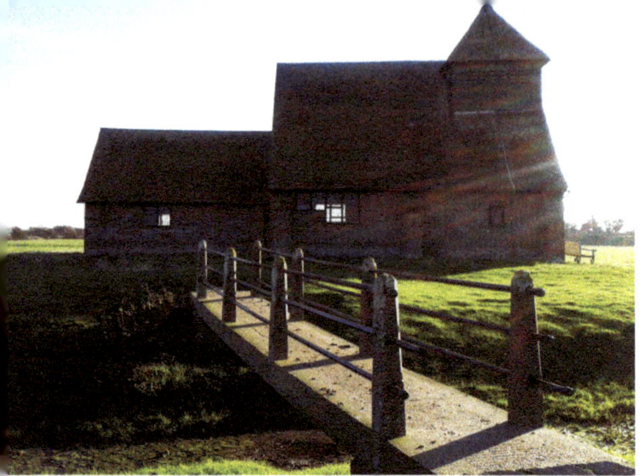
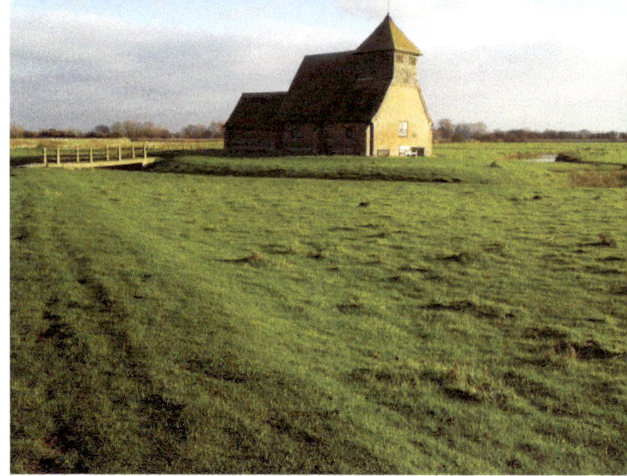
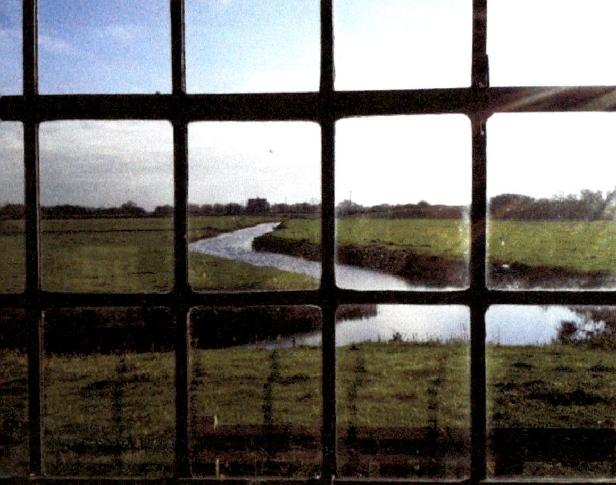

3. Ruins of Hope All Saints Church

There's not much to see at Hope, which is what makes it such a poignant place to visit. There was once a manor house at Hope, but now there is no sign of it. All that remains are a small collection of buildings, including a farm and the ruins of Hope All Saints Church. The church was built in the twelfth century by the lords of the manor for their own use and that of their tenants. It was still in use in 1541, but an archbishop's visit in 1575 found it decaying and in need of repair. By the eighteenth century the church was in ruins and was known locally as a meeting point for one of the smuggling gangs that virtually ruled Romney Marsh in those days.

This is not the only ruined church on Romney Marsh surrounded now only by fields. Similar ones are to be found at Midley, near Lydd, and Eastbridge, near Dymchurch, relics of now lost communities, the victims over the centuries of

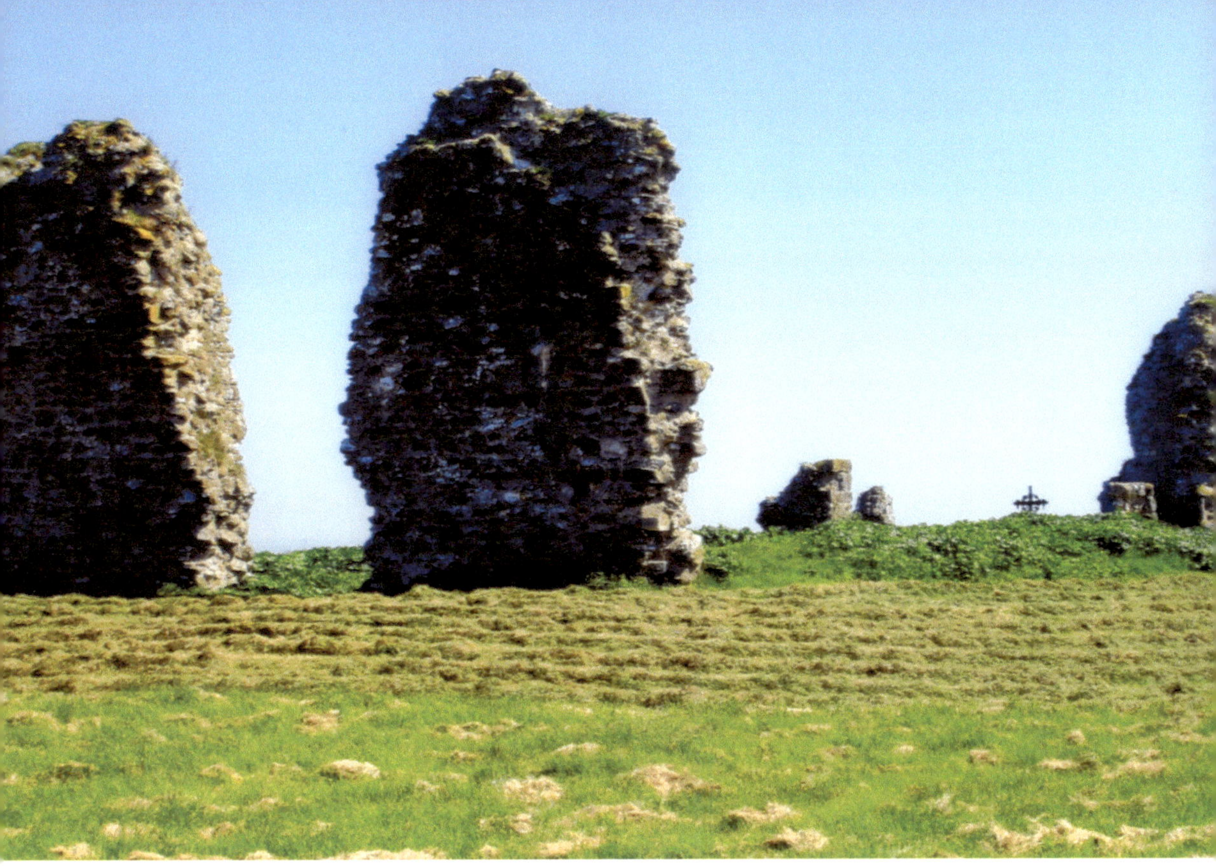

storms, plague, marsh ague (a once prevalent form of malaria) and the gradual decay of small rural communities over time.

Hope All Saints is perhaps the most visually striking of these ruined churches. When I first saw it from a distance it reminded me of my first view of Stonehenge. The ruins can be visited by the public and the land around is cared for by the current owners, who have also established an interesting small sculpture park nearby. Hope All Saints can be found just north of New Romney on the Ashford Road.

4. Dymchurch

Back on the coast heading north-east we come to the bustling, cheerful little seaside resort of Dymchurch. First impressions are all buckets and spades, funfair rides, amusement arcades, candy floss, donkey rides and miles of golden sandy beaches – the ideal traditional seaside holiday resort in miniature. As you

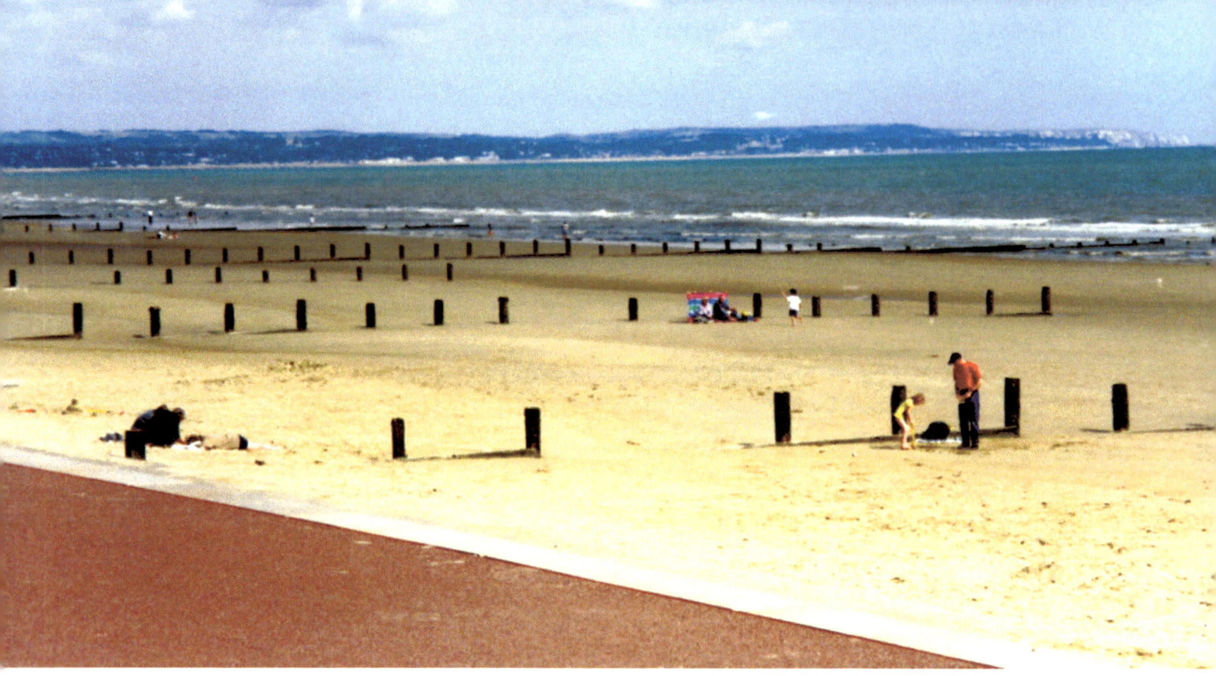

can imagine this is popular with families staying at the nearby holiday and caravan parks, particularly those with small children. An added attraction is the Romney, Hythe and Dymchurch Railway (RHDR), which can be boarded here for trips to Hythe or in the other direction to New Romney and Dungeness. For the adults there are busy pubs, restaurants, cafés and takeaways. It is all a great deal of fun, especially over the August bank holiday weekend when the Day of Syn festival is held. This relates to the smuggling history of Dymchurch and its fictional incarnation in the stories of the vicar-cum-smuggling gang leader Doctor Syn in a series of books by local author Russell Thorndike, two of which have been made into films.

Out of season Dymchurch seems more sedate, but still has a rich history to explore. A Dymchurch Heritage Trail takes visitors around the various points of interest in the village. These include the old courtroom and gaol at the New Hall, from where the 'Lords of the Level' once administered justice across Romney Marsh; the Norman St Peter and St Paul's Church next door; Martello Tower 24, run by English Heritage, which recreates what such a tower would have been like when in use as a defensive fort against the anticipated invasion by Napoleon in the early nineteenth century (it can be visited between Easter and October, on special open days or by arrangement); and the house where various notable residents lived at different times – i.e. playwright Noel Coward, authors Edith Nesbit and Russell Thorndike, and artist Paul Nash.

One of the public houses, the Ship Inn, dates back to 1452 and became a well-used smugglers pub centuries later. Russell Thorndike used to sit in the bar here writing his *Doctor Syn* novels and got some of the names for his characters from the gravestones in the churchyard of St Peter and St Paul's directly across the road.

When I lived for a few years on Romney Marsh at nearby St Mary's Bay, I used to like to walk to Dymchurch along the sea wall. Compared to St Mary's Bay, which is composed of mostly modern housing estates, Dymchurch seemed a lively metropolis. Here I would buy a paper, have a breakfast (or, if later, lunch), look in the second-hand bookshop for interesting bargains and enjoy convivial company in the local pubs – yes, to me it was, and is, definitely a gem.

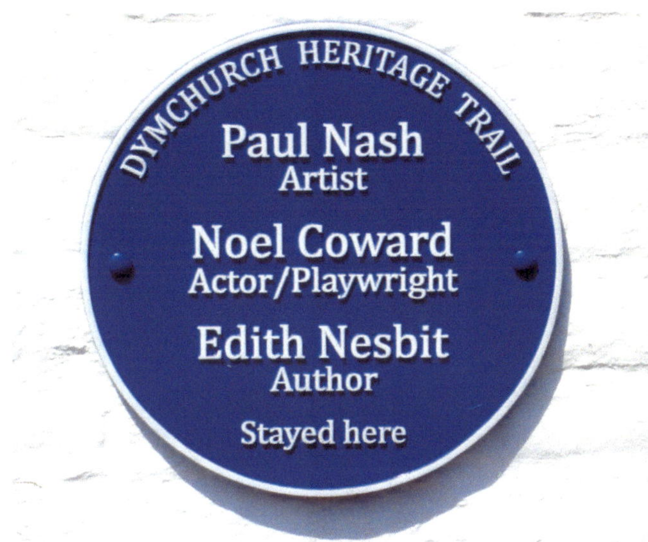

Right: On Dymchurch Heritage Trail.

Below: Parish church of St Peter and St Paul, Dymchurch.

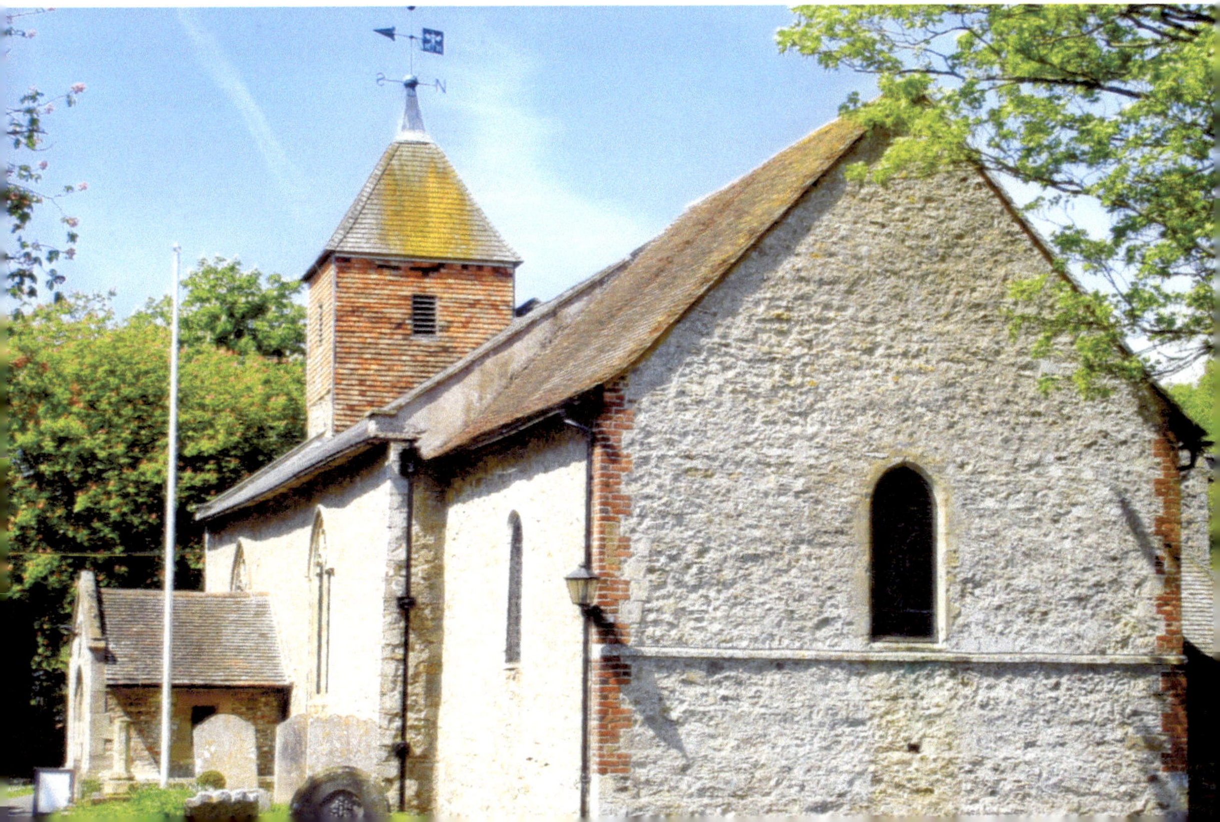

5. Port Lympne Wild Animal Park

Not far from Hythe, spread across 600 acres of mostly open countryside on the south-facing escarpment behind Romney Marsh, is the Port Lympne Wild Animal Park. This is one of those places you could easily spend a whole day exploring, and is very family friendly. At its centre is the mansion house and gardens built originally for the MP Sir Philip Sassoon in 1922. The estate was purchased in 1973 by John Aspinall to provide more room for his growing collection of wild animals, formerly confined just to the 90 acres of the Howletts Zoo Park at Bekesbourne, near Canterbury. Howletts opened to the public in 1975, and Port Lympne the following year.

At Port Lympne you can not only wander about the extensive grounds looking at animals in their enclosures, but also board trucks that will take you on a tour around the park's several zones, each dedicated to different continents – Africa, Asia and South America. Here you can see giraffes, zebra, black rhino, various antelope and deer, wildebeest, Bactrian camels, ostriches and many other creatures at close quarters, wandering free in a Kentish version of their natural habitat. The park also has the UK's largest gorillarium and home to a large breeding group of western lowland gorillas. In common with a number of such parks and always popular with children in particular, there are life-sized dinosaur models to be seen in an area known as 'Dinosaur Forest'. Some of these

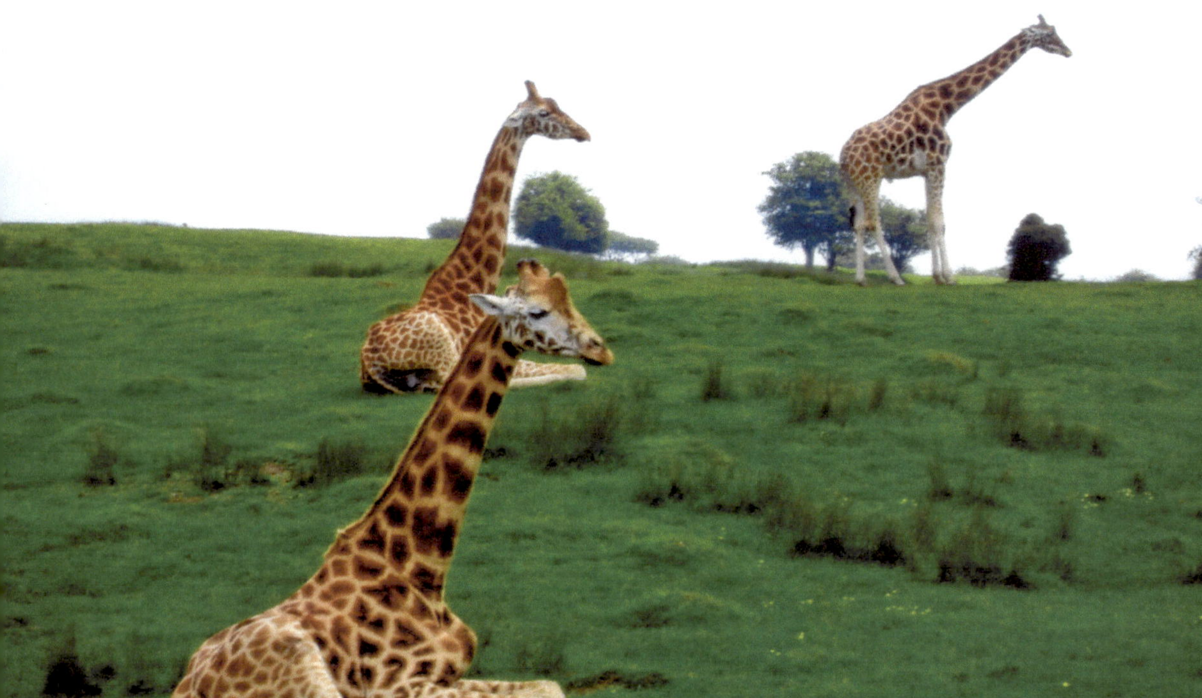

Giraffes at Port Lympne Wild Animal Park.

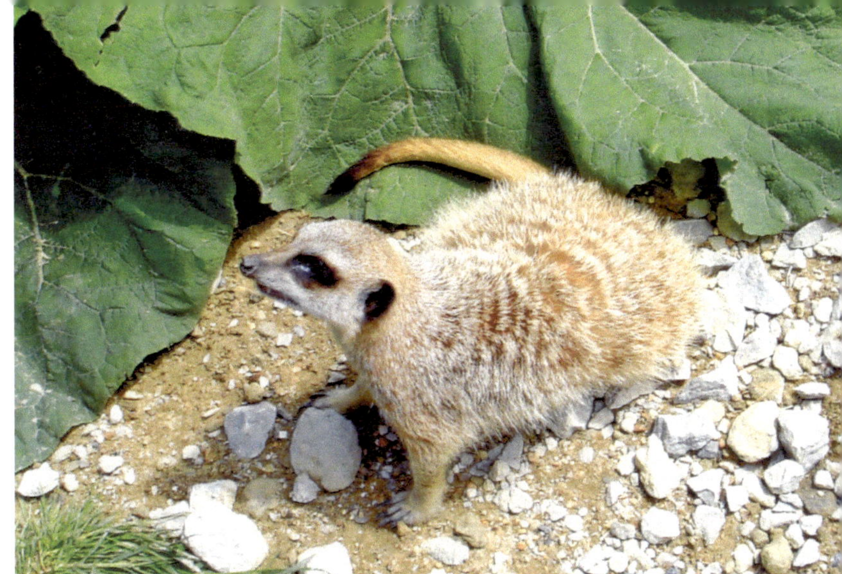

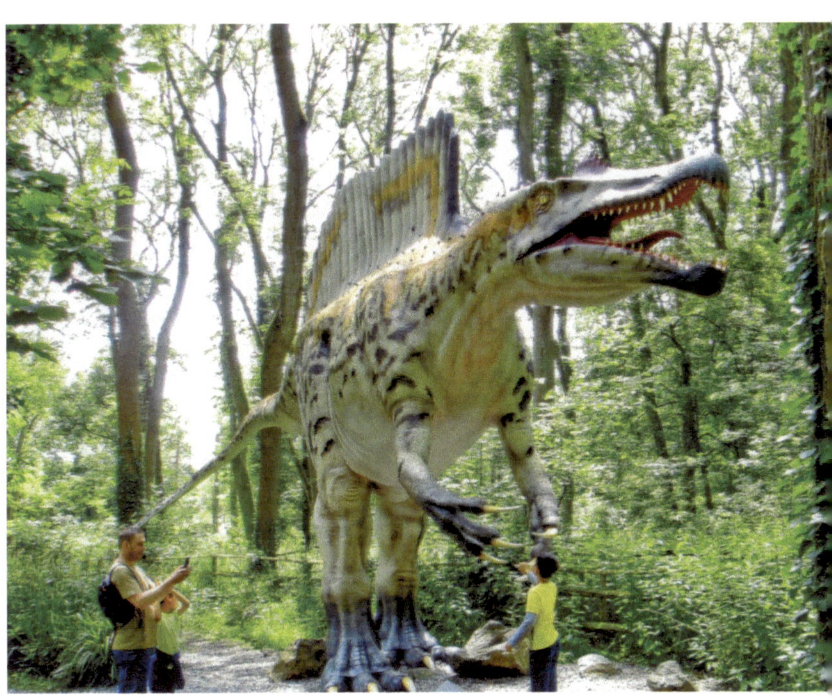

type of displays elsewhere can be a bit tacky, but not here at Port Lympne. The dinosaurs are numerous on quite a long woodland walk, with some emerging from the trees unexpectedly as you round a corner, being well camouflaged until you see them. Most of the main species of dinosaur are represented.

Port Lympne Wild Animal Park is not just a visitor attraction, it also does valuable conservation work and hosts some 700 species of rare and endangered animals. Particularly successful here have been the largest breeding herd of black rhinoceros in the UK and the successful reintroductions of these creatures back into the wild.

6. Portus Lemanis (Stutfall Castle)

Just east of Port Lympne Wild Animal Park lies what is left of the Portus Lemanis itself, the Roman fortified port that formed part of the Saxon Shore network of defensive structures erected in the third and fourth centuries AD. The scattering of broken and tumbled masonry to be seen on the escarpment overlooking Romney Marsh today is all that is left of a once proud Roman structure, a fortified base for the Classis Britannica, whose brief was to defend the Channel coast and seaways from the unwelcome attention of Saxon pirates.

Portus Lemanis probably saw action between AD 287 and 296 at a time of civil war within the Roman Empire as a result of the commander of the fleet, Carausius, seizing power over Britain and Gaul in AD 286. Excavations here have revealed abundant coins, mostly from this time, indicating it was much frequented during those ten years. The cessation of the coin series after AD 296 coincides with the reinvasion of Britain by imperial forces under Constantius Chlorus and the defeat of the rebellion.

Later, during the Saxon period the fort became known as Stutfall, which means 'stout wall', and was used as an enclosure to corral horses and cattle. Then, sometime between 975 and 1100 a landslip tore the walls asunder, leaving them in the state of disarray we see today. Later, in the twelfth to thirteenth centuries, stonework from the ruins was taken to help in the construction of

Ruins of Portus Lemanis/Stutfall Castle.

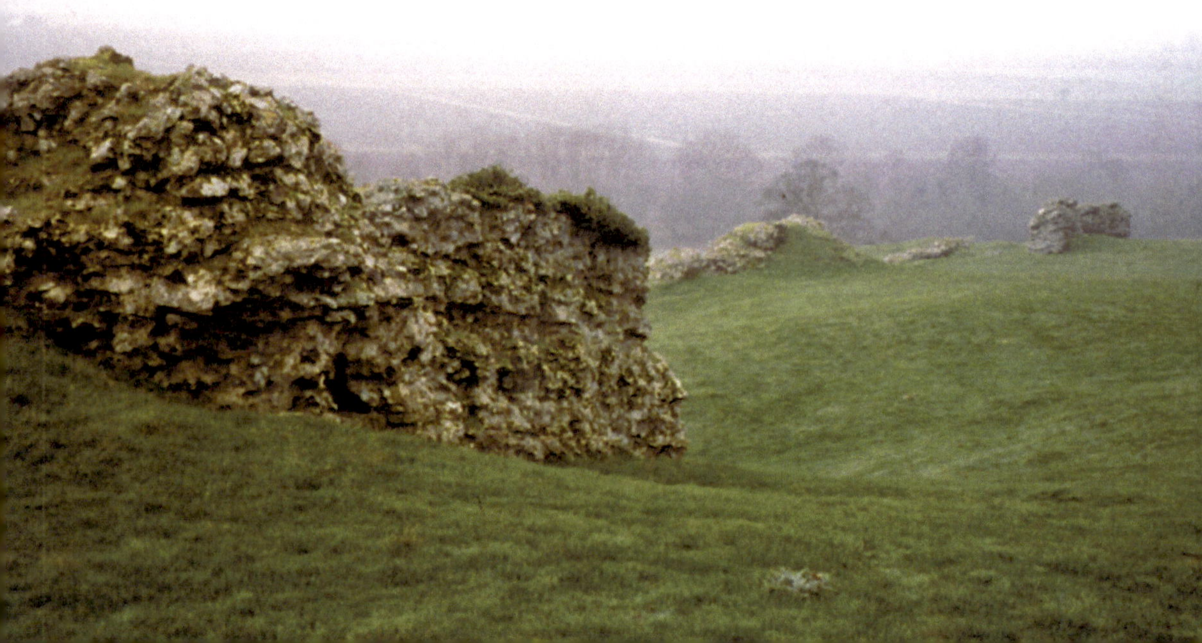

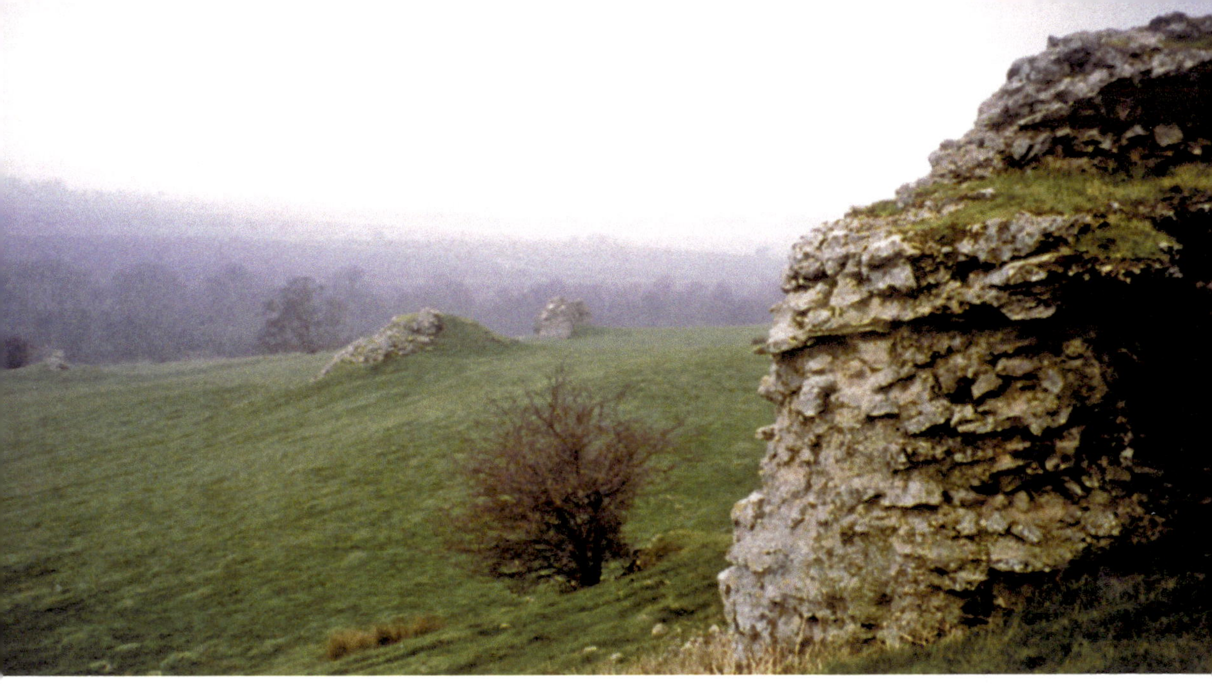

Lympne Castle, which stands on the crest of the ridge above and inland of the Roman site. Since then, this once mighty example of the power of Rome has lain abandoned, frequented only by sheep and the occasional walker, a reminder of how the constructions of humankind eventually succumb to nature and the march of time, a lesson in impermanence.

I first came across Stutfall Castle at the age of sixteen when I was studying *Macbeth* for O-level English Literature. Our school, in its wisdom, decided that it would help us learn if we made a film of the play, with us in the various parts. I was Banquo and accompanied Macbeth on his first visit to the three witches, who in our film cavorted to great effect around the ruins of Stutfall Castle. You couldn't hope for a better location and it looked quite the part in our Super 8-mm film, though I remember the sound recording didn't quite synchronise some of the time.

You can see the ruins of Stutfall Castle from the footpath that leads west on the inland side of the Royal Military Canal. It is a short walk up the escarpment to the ruins.

7. Romney, Hythe and Dymchurch Railway

The Romney, Hythe and Dymchurch Railway (RHDR) is said to be the smallest public railway service in the world. The line, which opened in 1927, was the brainchild of three men, Henry Greenly, Captain J. E. P. Howey and the racing driver Louis Zborowski (who was tragically killed in motor racing accident before he could see his dream realised).

The miniature rail line uses one third full-size steam and diesel locomotives along 13.5 miles of track that runs between Hythe and Dungeness stopping at Dymchurch, Romney Warren, New Romney and Greatstone in between. As well as taking tourists on pleasure trips, the railway also provides a regular commuter service for schoolchildren from across the Marsh.

There is a lot to see on the route of the RHDR if you use it as a sort of spine from which to branch out and visit different places across Romney Marsh. Starting at the ancient cinque port of Hythe, a pretty town with its traditional high street, canal walks and St Leonard's Church crypt (more on this later),

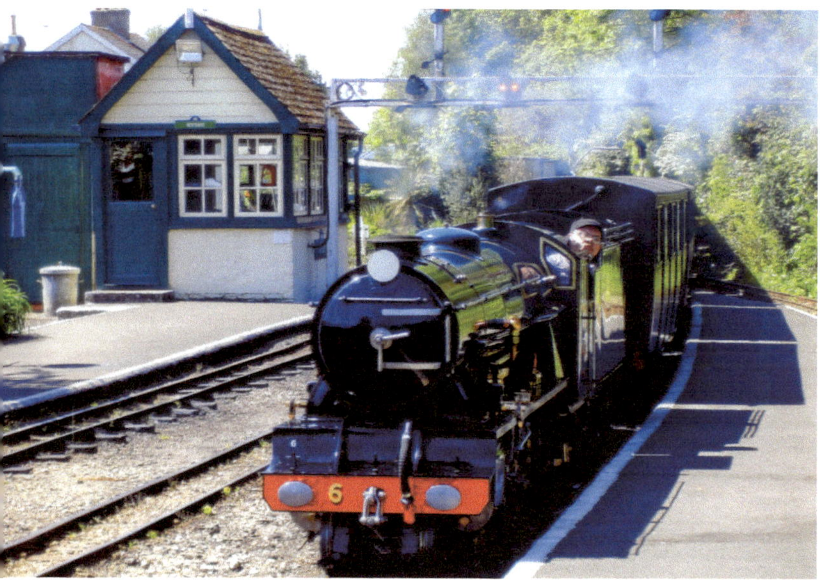

RHDR steam locomotive arriving at Hythe.

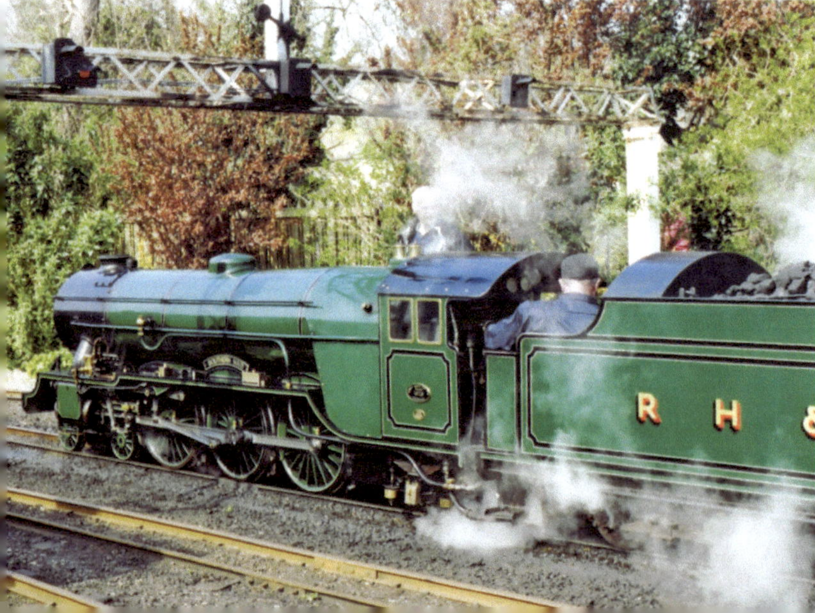

RHDR steam locomotive setting out for Dungeness. (Photo by Candida Wright)

the line heads south-west to Dymchurch. After this there is Romney Warren, a new stop allowing passengers to get off and explore the Romney Marsh Visitor Centre and the surrounding Romney Warren Nature Reserve. New Romney is the next stop, a larger, busy station also housing a model railway exhibition. The town itself has a full range of shops and the church of St Nicholas, where you can see the tide marks left by a tidal surge resulting from a devastating storm in 1287 that redrew the map of Romney Marsh forever. Greatstone is next, a holiday camp and extensive golden sands. Land yachting can be watched or undertaken here. The final stop is Dungeness. There is a good week's worth of pleasant exploring, chuffing up and down the line on this little train.

8. Royal Military Canal

If you are in Hythe on a sunny, pleasant day you might be well advised to take a walk along the towpath of the Royal Military Canal, which runs the length of the town and on for a total of 28 miles to Cliff End in East Sussex. Of course, you can do the whole 28-mile walk if so inclined, looking out for kingfishers, grey herons and mute swans, listening to birdsong or the distinctive 'chuckling' of the large green marsh frog (often nicknamed the 'laughing frog'), or just soak up the relaxing atmosphere on the way. In Hythe itself the canal banks have been turned into a pleasant linear town park.

Royal Military Canal at Hythe.

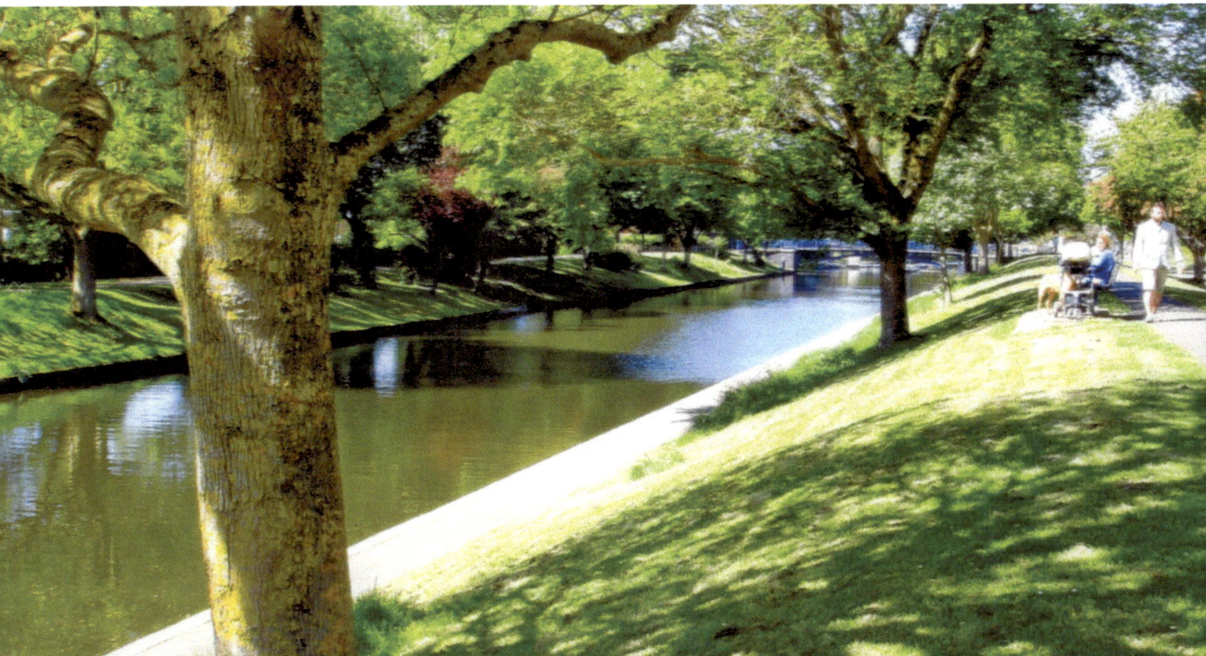

The Royal Military Canal was dug by hand by hundreds of labourers. Work began in 1804 and was completed in 1809, the canal being a defensive measure against an expected invasion by the French under Napoleon, along with the string of Martello towers that can be found along the coast of southern and eastern England. This was not just a defensive ditch; after all, if Napoleon had crossed the Channel and got past the Royal Navy a 19-metre-wide water-filled ditch might not be expected to hold him back. Was this literally a 'last ditch' line of defence then? Not at all, the canal would have been used to allow British troops to travel with ease up and down the length of Romney Marsh to engage Napoleon's forces wherever they had decided to land on this low-lying and vulnerable coastline. Fortunately the anticipated invasion never came, and the Royal Military Canal became considered a monumental waste of money.

Today, however, it is an important nature reserve with a long-distance walk and leisure facilities at the Hythe end – such as boat trips and rowing boats or kayaks for hire. There is even a carnival every two years along the length of the canal at Hythe, known as the Hythe Venetian Fête, which is famous for the quality of its floats.

9. St Leonard's Church, Hythe

St Leonard's is an interesting church, standing imposingly on the escarpment behind Hythe. It is of Norman construction with, it was once claimed by Professor Francis Bond, 'the finest chancel of any church in England, not to say Europe!' The churchyard contains the graves of no less than Lionel Lukin, who patented the world's first lifeboat in 1785, and Francis Petit Smith, the inventor of the screw propeller. It is the crypt of this fine church, though, that really draws people in.

The crypt, also known as the 'House of Bones', contains numerous skulls and thigh bones – all neatly stacked. It is thought that the remains of between 2,000 and 4,000 people are stored here. The most likely explanation is that the bones and skulls are the result of the graveyard being cleared of remains between the thirteenth and fifteenth centuries to make room for the extension of the church and for new burials. There is no evidence to suggest that these are the bones of battle victims, as some have guessed. A total of 50 per cent of the bones are female and 10 per cent are child remains, and they seem, in most cases, to have died from natural causes and to have been a normal cross section of the community. The bones provide an interesting view into the health of Hythe's population during the medieval period. Osteoarthritis, poor dental hygiene and anaemia are all in evidence, though many of the skulls indicate teeth in good condition despite being somewhat worn down from eating coarse food. The crypt's limited opening hours are displayed at the church, which is open every day.

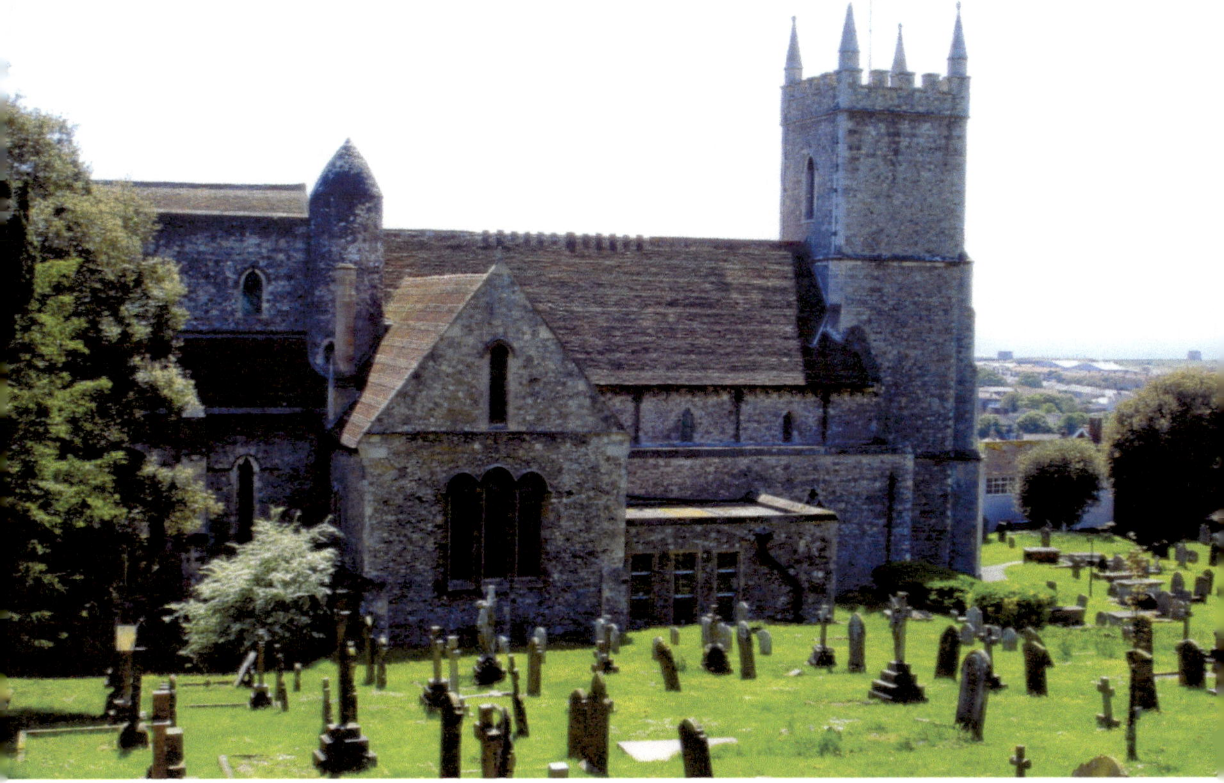

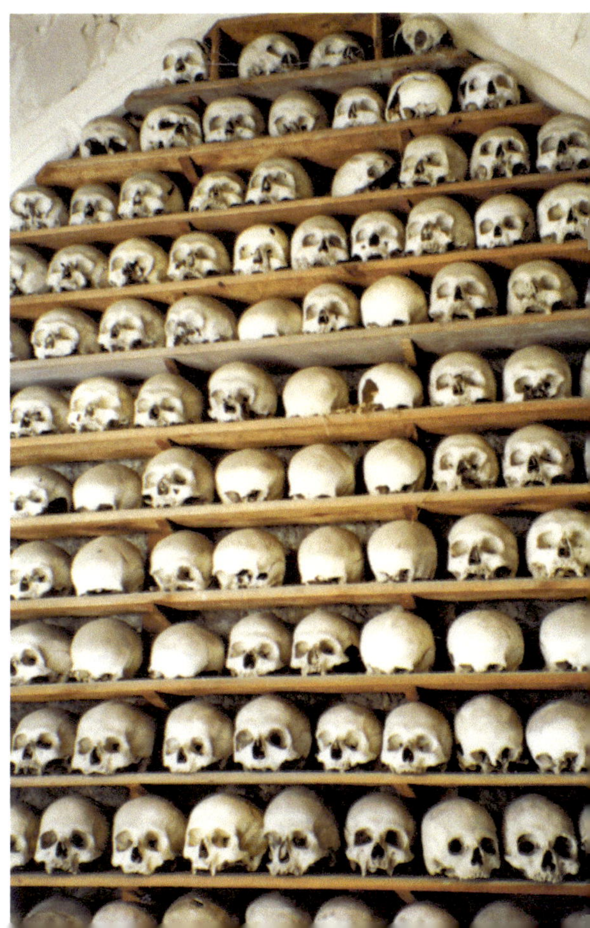

Above: St Leonard's Church, Hythe.

Right: Skulls in the crypt of St Leonard's Church, Hythe.

10. Sandgate

East of Hythe we come to the pleasant seaside village of Sandgate, with its busy little High Street sporting antique shops, pleasant pubs with good food and real ale, an interesting old fire station that acts as a museum for the Sandgate Society, and a parallel sea wall bordered by many pleasant villas and cottages.

The hills behind Sandgate are wooded and laced with footpaths. Hidden among the trees are ruined Martello towers covered in ivy, abandoned like lost fairy tale castles. In contrast to this, not far away stands the massive glass castle housing the Saga Company's headquarters, towering over the eastern end of the village. On the seafront is Sandgate Castle, built in 1539 as one of Henry VIII's fortifications to deter a popish invasion following his falling out with the Catholic authorities in Rome. This has since been developed into a Martello tower, was converted later into a restaurant and is now a private house. The images on the village sign sum up the main visible features of the place, but don't hint at its literary past.

Just up the hill towards Folkestone, Wells House Nursing Home occupies what was once Spade House, built for H. G. Wells in 1900 and the place where some of his best-known novels were written. While there, Wells entertained a number of well-known writers of the time, such as George Bernard Shaw, Henry James and Joseph Conrad. It has been suggested that during Wells's time here (1900–09) Sandgate became the literary hub of the western world. Wells's novel *The First Men in the Moon* (1901) was published while he was at Spade House and parts of it were set on the Kent coast. *The Sea Lady* (1902) was largely set in Sandgate and the popular novel *Kipps* (1905), perhaps best known today for having been adapted in the musical *Half A Sixpence* (1968), is set largely in Folkestone.

Just along the road called Radnor Cliff, a short distance and a few years later, lived the underrated exquisitely articulate and humorous writer Jocelyn Brooke, author of *The Military Orchid* (1948) and *The Dog at Clambercrown* (1955), but we'll speak more about him in a later entry.

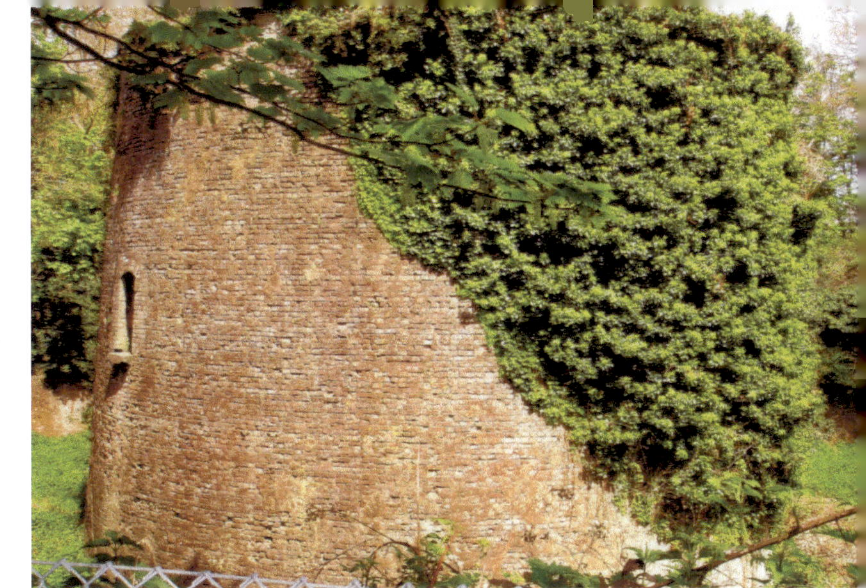

Martello towers in the woods behind Sandgate.

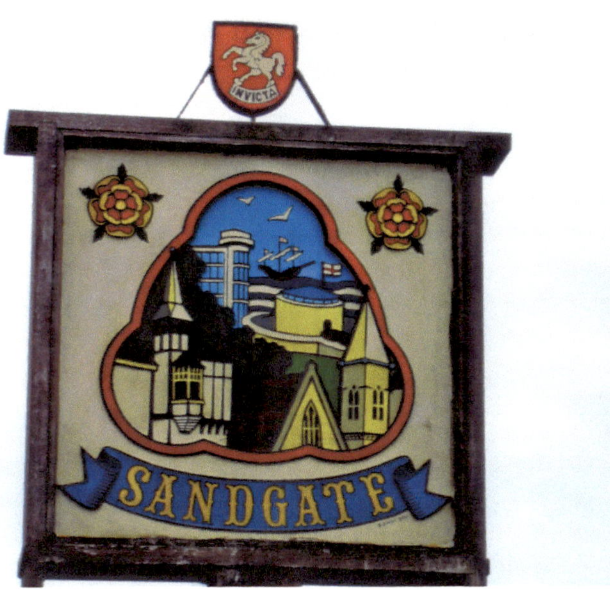

Sandgate village sign.

11. The Leas and Coastal Park

Along the clifftop from Sandgate to Folkestone runs the Leas, once described as the 'finest marine promenade in the world'. This is a mile-long stretch of lawns and sea views backed by palatial buildings from Folkestone's Victorian and Edwardian heyday such as the red-brick and terracotta Metropole and the Grand, the latter much frequented by Edward VII when it was a gentleman's club and apartments. Both buildings became hotels and are now largely quality apartments, with entertainment and function rooms at the Grand. Further east are the impressive Burlington Hotel and the Manor House, the latter once home to the Earl of Radnor, as the name suggests. Then there is an ornate bandstand, the Leas Cliff Hall entertainment venue and an impressive memorial arch to those who fell in the First World War, which was opened by Prince Harry in 2014.

Parallel to the Leas, down at shore level, stretches the Lower Leas Coastal Park, described by Sarah Guy in her recent book *London on Sea* as the 'jewel in Folkestone's crown'. Here you can wander in formal gardens at the eastern end, keep children entertained in the 'fun zone' (a large outdoor adventure playground)

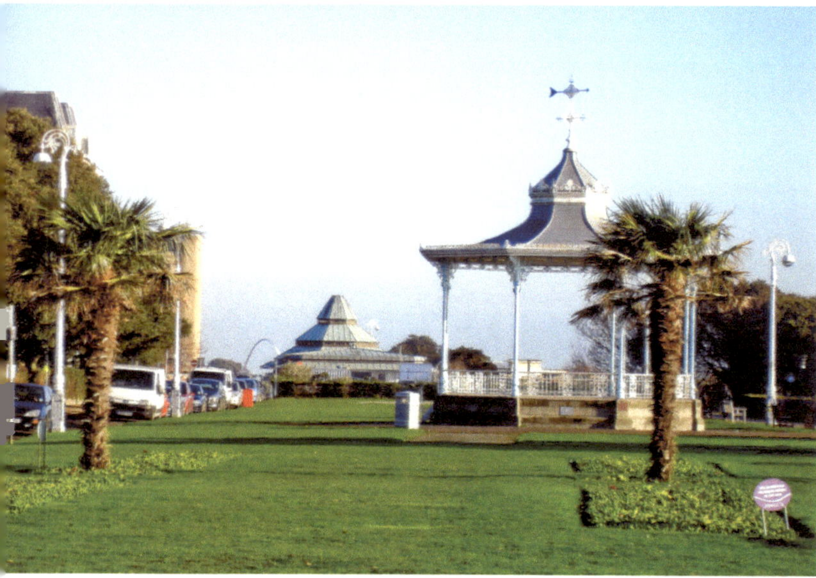

The Leas showing bandstand, Leas Cliff Hall and distant Memorial Arch.

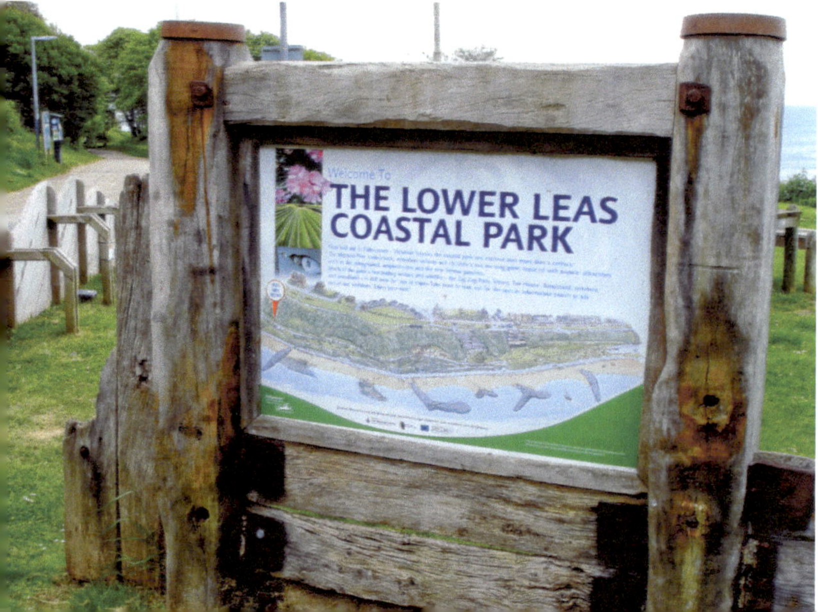

Western (Sandgate) entrance to the Lower Leas Coastal Park.

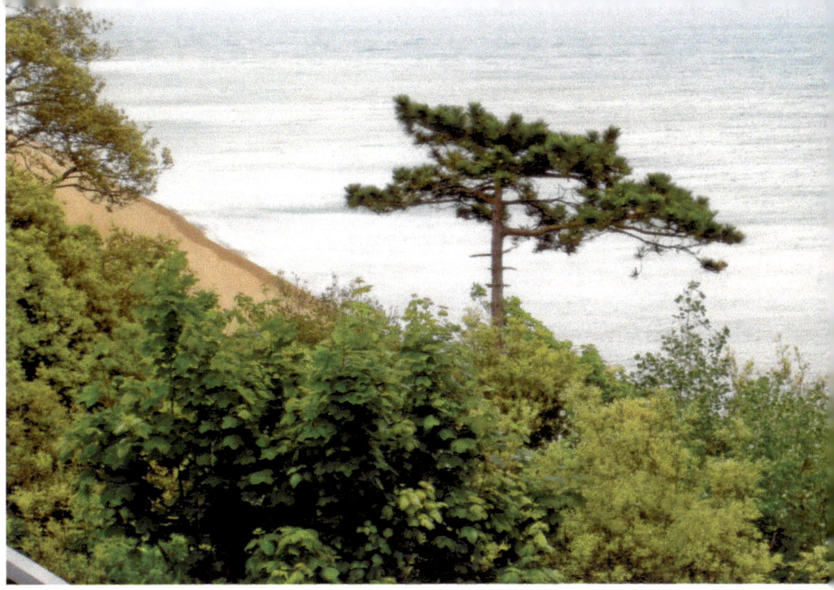

or picnic in the pleasant wooded glades of the 'wild zone' at the park's western end. In the Lower Leas Coastal Park you can be among greenery and by the sea, a winning combination. The beach is mostly single with sheltered bays, one of which for several years recently was occupied by a dolphin affectionately known as Dave. The park holds the coveted Green Flag award – recognition that this is one of the country's best parks.

The coastal park can be seen from the Leas and a number of paths and steps connect the two through the cliffside woods. At the eastern end of the Leas, near the Memorial Arch, is a water balance lift known as the Leas Lift. Currently this is mothballed pending refurbishment, but hopefully will be taking people up and down the cliffs again in the not too distant future.

12. Zig Zag Path, Folkestone

A particular feature of the connection between the Leas and the Lower Leas Coastal Park is the Zig Zag Path, which starts near the bandstand and descends through arches, caves and grottoes to the park below. It reaches the coastal park at the transition point between the 'formal zone' of landscaped gardens and the 'fun zone', where the children's adventure playground is. Here at the bottom of the patch is an amphitheatre, popular for shows and performances in the summer (I have watched two Shakespeare plays here).

The Zig Zag Path itself is perhaps not what it appears. The cliffs down which the path descends and the caves through which it passes are not a natural feature. The original cliff is sandstone, but the stone facing through which the path passes is a conglomerate of concrete and various other substances and items that have created an interesting granite-like appearance and hardness. This mixture was the invention of a John Pulham and so is known as 'Pulhamite'.

Pulham was responsible for the construction of this Zig Zag Path as a scheme to provide work for unemployed labourers in 1922, when what we now know as the coastal park was first laid out on the natural landslip-created shelf that runs along the bottom of these cliffs. The current layout of the coastal park was completed in 2001, with additional improvements in subsequent years. It is a beautiful, relaxing place with the quiet, magical Zig Zag Path as a portal through which to approach it.

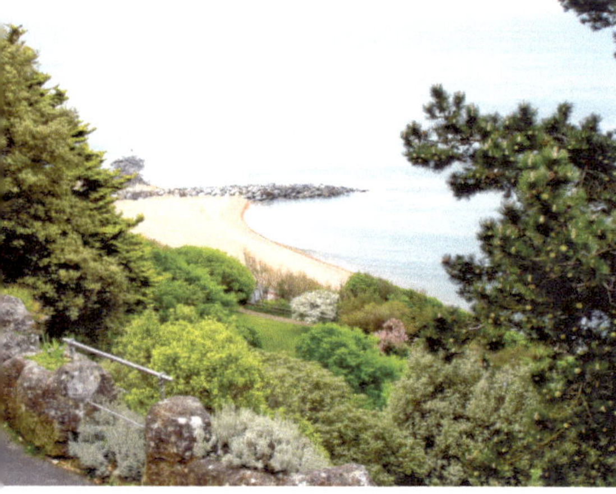

Zig Zag Path leading down to Coastal Path.

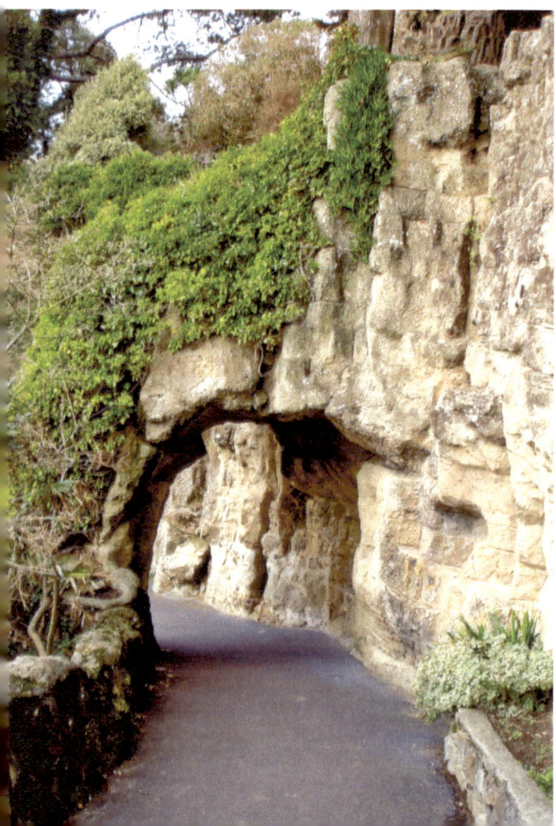

A Zig Zag Path tunnel.

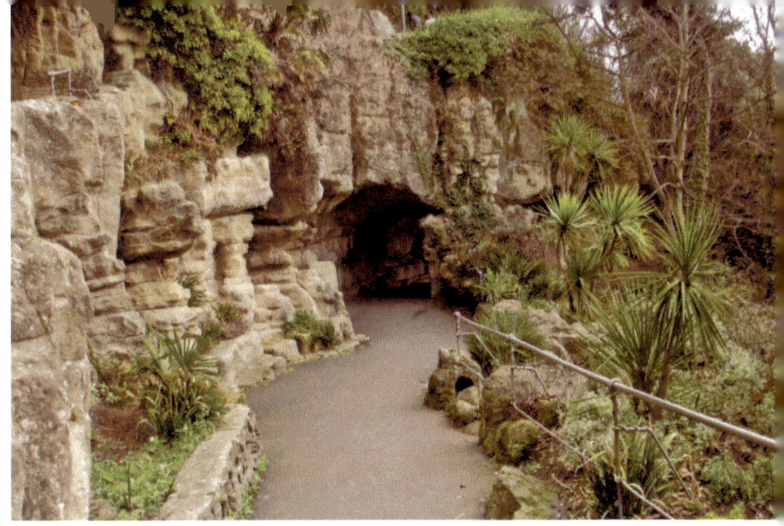

13. St Mary and St Eanswythe's Church, Folkestone

Folkestone's parish church not only has a beautiful interior but also contains what are believed to be the relics of its founding saint, Eanswythe. Eanswythe is believed to have founded England's first nunnery near here in around AD 630, and was credited with a number of miracles as well. Perhaps best known of these is the bringing of fresh water by means of a watercourse from the hills behind the town. Legend tells us that this stream passed through another 'unmingled' before reaching its destination at the nunnery, all traces of which have now disappeared. Local historian Eamonn Rooney helpfully pointed out to me that on a Radnor Estate map of 1698 the stream indicated on 'St Eanswythe's Watercourse' is shown passing over another on its journey from the freshwater springs of the hills by means of what the map describes as a 'wooden trough'. It seems the watercourse was a contour aqueduct and the basis for this legend. A project is underway at the time of writing to investigate this and other aspects of the Eanswythe legend using modern archaeological research techniques. The relics of St Eanswythe were rediscovered in 1885, having been hidden near the altar at the time of the Reformation. Folkestone is only one of two parish churches in the country to still have the relics of their founding saint – the other being the church of St Candida and Holy Cross at Morcombelake in Dorset.

Aside from the legend of St Eanswythe, the parish church of St Mary and St Eanswythe is a gem in its own right. Although a church was established in Eanswythe's time this has long ago disappeared, but was replaced eventually by King Athelstan in the year 929. This lasted until 1052 when it was destroyed by Earl Godwin in a raid on Folkestone, part of a disagreement he was having with

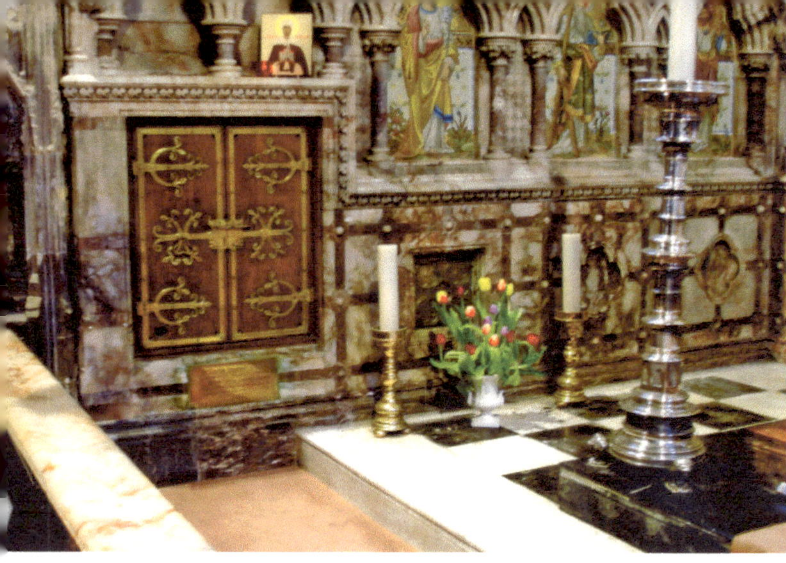

Edward the Confessor at the time. The present church was founded in 1138 and the current dedication made. Not very much of the early building survives as there have been refurbishments in the centuries since. The interior of this church today presents a very interesting and beautiful sight, largely the result of work by the Canon Mathew Woodward, whose incumbency lasted from 1851 to 1898 and during whose time Eanswythe's relics were found.

The atmosphere in this church is beautifully tranquil, particularly in the Lady Chapel and near the shrine and altar. I have known this church since I used to come here as a primary school pupil and still find it as awe inspiring as I did then.

14. Folkestone Harbour and Harbour Arm

This forms the vibrant hub of seaside activity in Folkestone, particularly on fine days. Folkestone Harbour as we see it today consists of an inner tidal harbour where fishing boats and yachts anchor and the Harbour Arm, where the Channel ferries used to dock but now has a new role as a popular food, drink and entertainment venue.

Around the inner harbour, which dates back to 1809, are pubs, seafood stalls, ice creams, souvenirs, a sandy beach (at the eastern end) overlooked by a sculpture called *The Folkestone Mermaid*, fish 'n' chips, a sea sports centre and the famous quality waterfront restaurant Rocksalt. A viaduct that once took boat trains to the ferry terminal on the Harbour Arm is now a pedestrian walkway crossing the inner harbour and providing seating and good coastal views, particularly to the east.

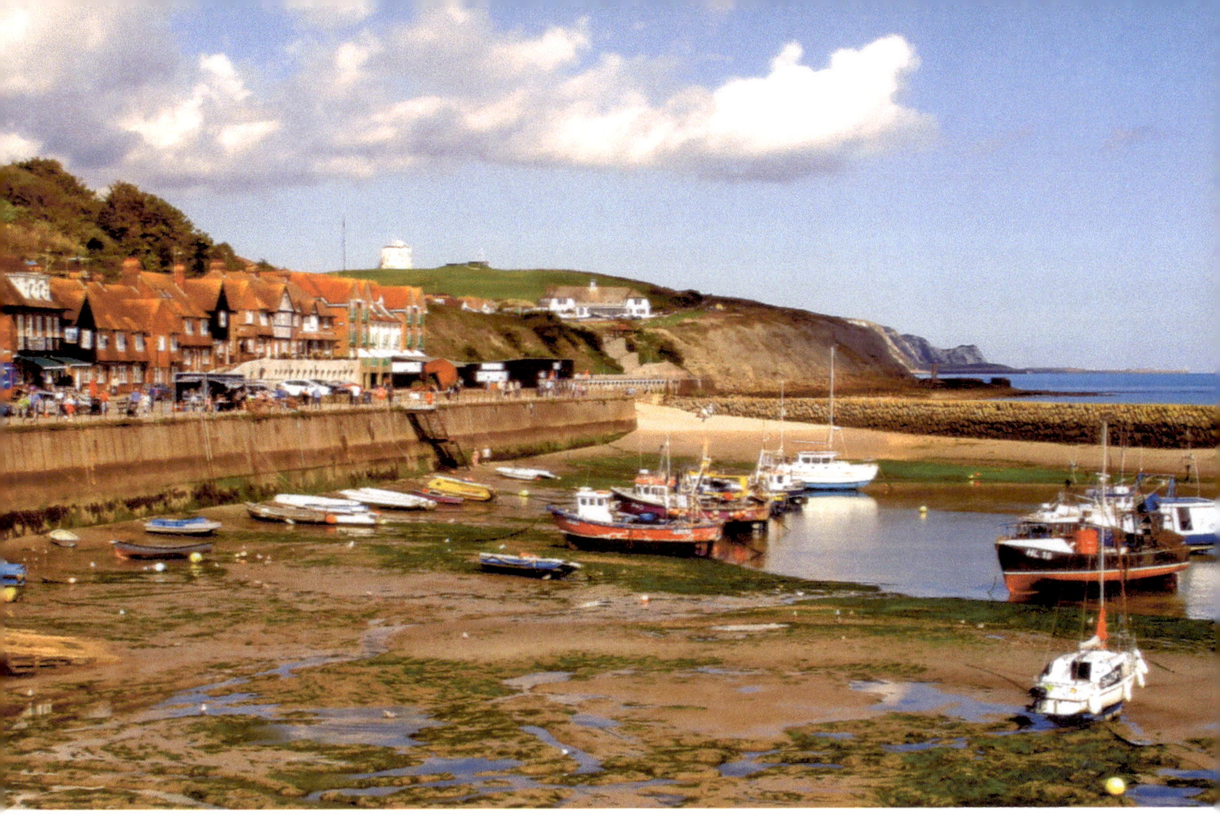

Folkestone Inner Harbour from the viaduct.

The Harbour Arm is accessed from the viaduct footway and stretches far out to the sea, providing, in effect, a substantial pier-type facility for the town. In 1849, the first popular cross-Channel ferry service ran from here over to Boulogne. In the First World War this was the main embarkation point for British troops bound for the battlefields of Europe. The ferries and boat trains have long gone as a result of the coming of the Channel Tunnel, and later the end of duty-free shopping. Now, though, the Harbour Arm is enjoying a new lease of life as a leisure facility. The old rail platforms have been refurbished, a large car park created and numerous small, quality food and drink outlets established in the old waiting rooms along with interesting kiosks along the length of the pier. Events including live music, firework displays and large outdoor screen film and sports event showings take place here for most of the year, though not in bad weather. There are excellent views from the Harbour Arm back towards the town and along the coast in both directions. I think this new attraction really sells Folkestone as a place to visit and perhaps to live and work in too. The town can be seen from the Harbour Arm in its true landscape setting.

At the end of the Harbour Arm stands a lighthouse, beneath which hides a small bar. What better place to sit outside on a warm summer evening with a cool drink and admire the stunning views? The Harbour Arm buzzes in fine weather with visitors and residents, including the many cosmopolitan and creative types that have brought new energy and ideas to Folkestone in recent years.

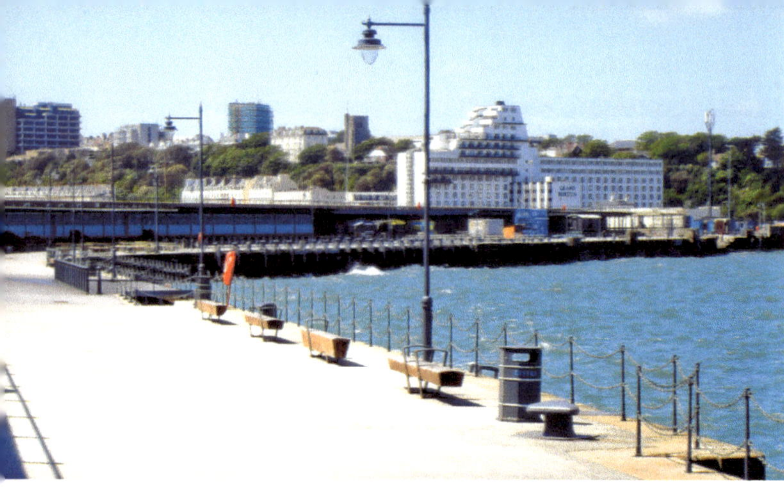

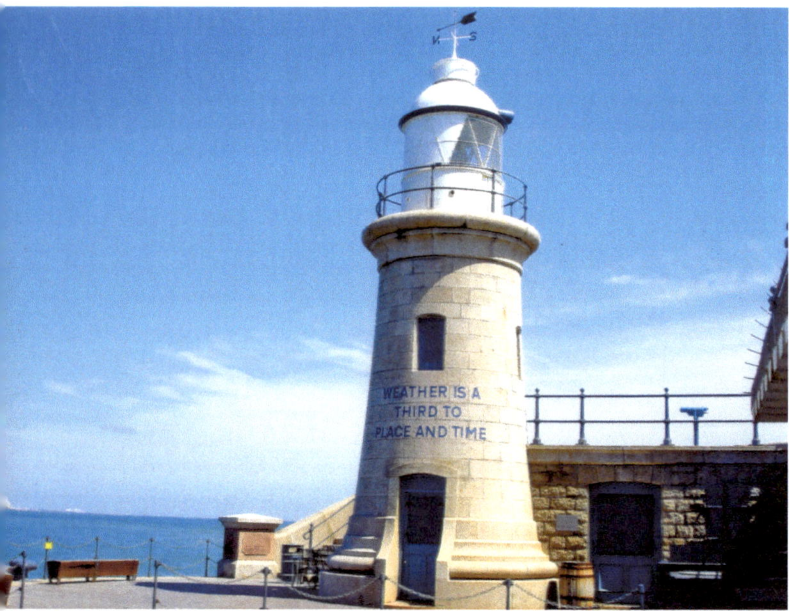

15. East Wear Bay/The Warren

To my mind, one of East Kent's most precious 'gems' in the natural history sphere is The Warren, also known as Folkestone Warren. This is a Site of Special Scientific Interest (SSSI) for a number of reasons – its geology, fossils, landscape features and natural history. This 7-mile-long nature reserve has distinct zones with particular characteristics. I think my favourite is East Wear Bay and its immediate hinterland. Here, gault clay cliffs tumble down to a rugged foreshore creating a chaotic terrain of landslip and undercliff, thickly vegetated in parts with hidden ponds in hollows and clefts that have become the home of newts, dragonflies, abundant horsetails and nesting moorhens. On the shore is the largest expanse of rocks and rock pools in the south-east of England (and now part of a Marine Conservation Zone), containing crabs, anemones and brittle stars and playing host to flocks of Mediterranean gulls that choose to roost here along with visiting grey and common seals that bob up from their underwater foraging from time to time. The mixed sand and rock shoreline has a wild look about it: trees tumble from the undercliff and lie bleached on the shoreline among the flotsam and jetsam. At the foot of the gault clay cliffs beautiful ammonites, belemnites and other Mesozoic fossils can be found washed out onto the beach. This rugged bay has been nicknamed 'Castaway Beach' recently by Irish dance artist Siobhan Ni Dhuinnin. I immediately related to this – East Wear Bay does indeed have a sort of *Robinson Crusoe* feel about it.

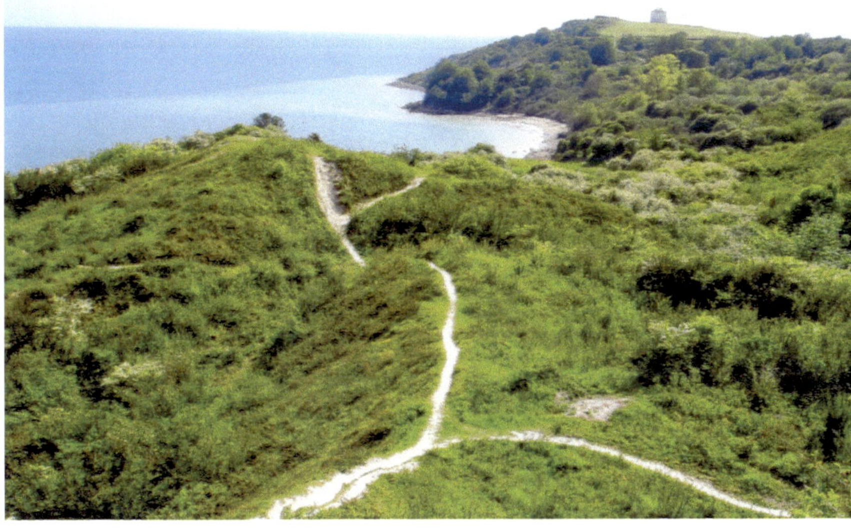

Folkestone Warren and East Wear Bay.

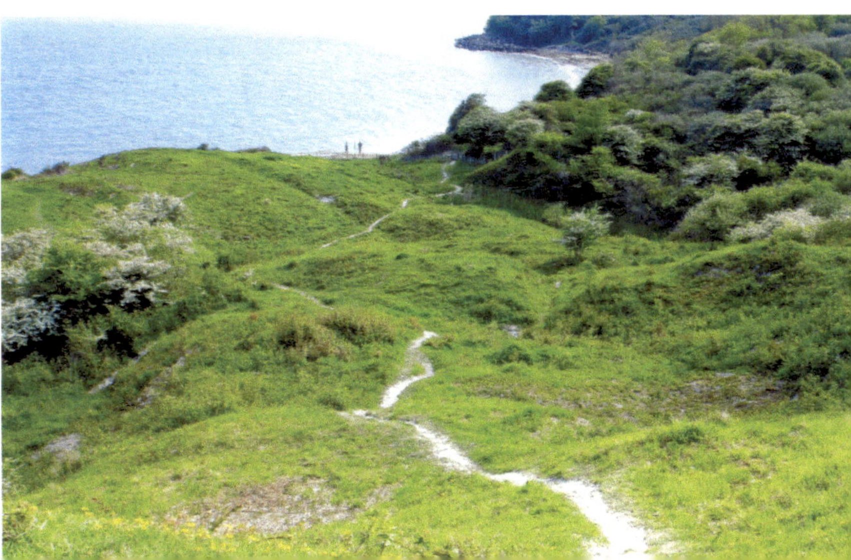

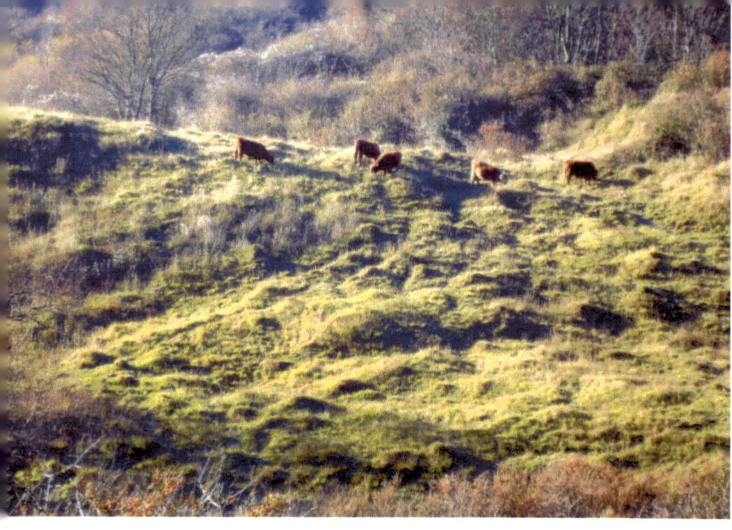

Just north-east and inland from 'Castaway Beach' the geology changes from gault clay to chalk and the scenery changes too. Small hills and valleys created by past landslips and laced with white paths winding among the turf and scrub bring to mind H. G. Wells's comment on the area in his popular novel *Kipps*. He describes The Warren as 'that queer little wilderness of slippery and tumbling clay and rock under the chalk cliffs, a wilderness of thorn and bramble, wild rose and wayfaring tree that adds so greatly to Folkestone's charm'.

Today around 20 acres of this area is being grazed by Highland cattle to reclaim lost grassland and allow a wider variety of plant and insect life to flourish. Judging by the number of common species spotted – lady, bee, pyramidal and late spider orchids have been found on these hills in late spring and early summer in recent years – it seems their grazing has had the desired effect.

16. Little Switzerland

Higher up in The Warren, near the base of 500-foot-high chalk cliffs, is one of the best viewpoints in the vicinity – conveniently the site of a café and camping site. This spot, which in my estimation is a separate 'gem' in itself, is known as Little Switzerland, and a good starting or finishing point for walks in the upper part of Folkestone Warren, north of the Folkestone to Dover railway line.

As well as good views and refreshments, this site is notable for its mysterious lizards. Reptile study groups have identified Italian wall lizards, which are to be found sunning themselves on stones, steps and acres of bare earth in warm weather. The lizards are of a beautifully green patterned appearance and emerge from holes in embankments and from underneath the ladies shower block in particular. The Kent Reptile and Amphibian Group (KRAG), estimated a few years ago there was a population of some 180 lizards. The campsite proprietor thinks there are now more than that. Similar lizards are also found in comparable areas along England's Channel coast and notably the landslip/undercliff areas of the south coast of the Isle of Wight. The mystery, of course, is where did they come from? Suggestions include surplus stock dumped by the pet trade, or that they have arrived hidden in tourist camper vans, subsequently finding a niche in the warm microclimate of these south-facing and vegetated cliffs and undercliffs.

From the tea chalet at Little Switzerland enticing views tempt the walker and paths lead down into the undercliff woodland where a green and primeval feeling environment shelters a carpet of hart's tongue ferns. The presence of this bright green woodland floor has led to these woods having become known, in recent years, as Hart's Tongue Wood.

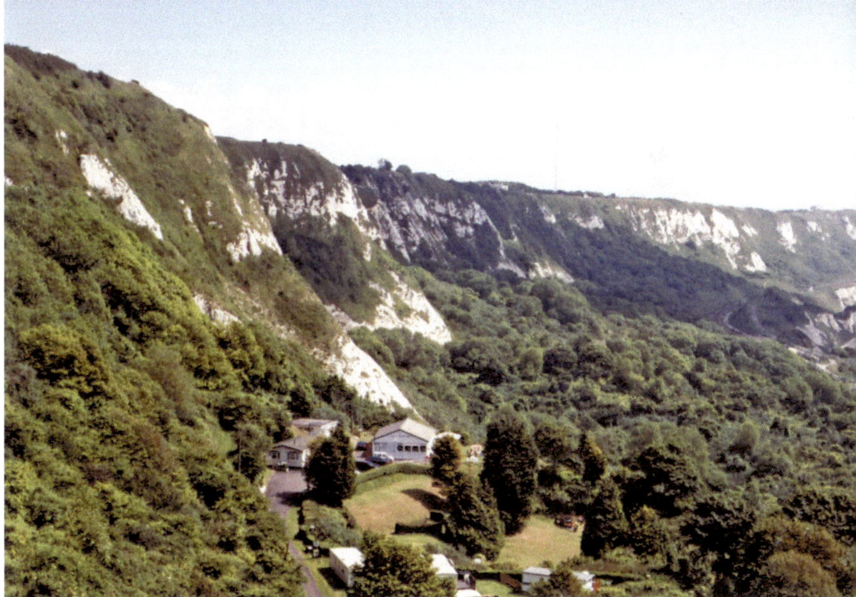

Little Switzerland and the Warren beyond.

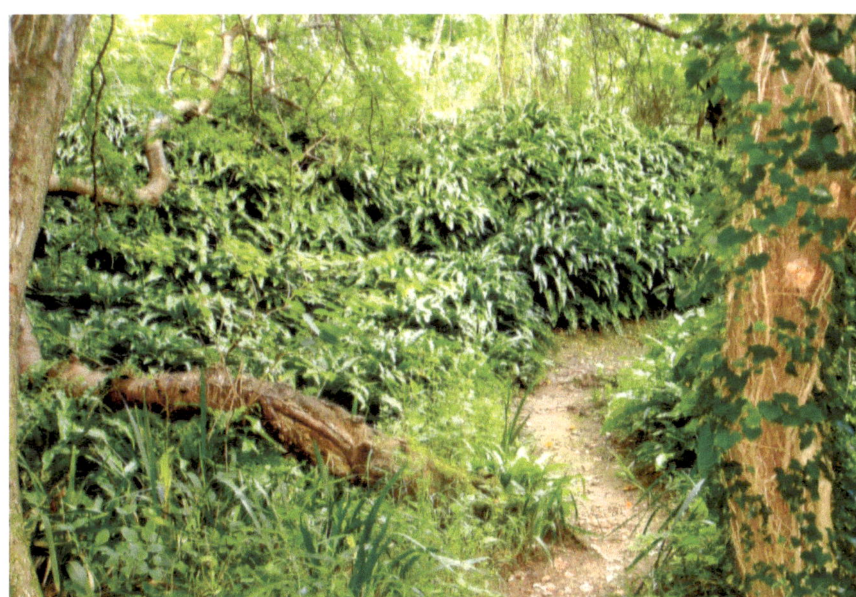

Hart's Tongue Wood.

17. Battle of Britain Memorial

Up above Little Switzerland on the clifftop at Capel-le-Ferne proudly stands the *National Memorial to the Few* – the Battle of Britain memorial. Centrepiece to the memorial is the statue of a Battle of Britain pilot sitting in the middle of a concrete structure, which, seen from above, forms the shape of an aircraft propeller. The statue was unveiled by HRH Queen Elizabeth the Queen Mother on 10 July 1993. Here, wreaths are laid on Memorial Day, which is held each year on a Sunday close to the date of the start of the famous battle. A flypast by the Battle of Britain memorial flight, which consists of a Spitfire, a Hurricane and a Lancaster bomber, takes place on this day. Spitfires are also sometimes seen flying overhead around the memorial on other summer weekends too. A replica Spitfire and Hurricane are situated in the grounds of the memorial.

'The Few' are the 2,937 airmen who made at least one operational sortie under the control of RAF Fighter Command between 10 July and 31 October 1940. They were entitled to wear the Battle of Britain clasp and their name carved on the black granite panels of the Christopher Foxley-Norris memorial wall that curves around the north end of the memorial site.

In 2015 a new feature opened at this atmospheric site. Known as 'The Wing', this is a visitor centre incorporating not only a gift shop, café and memorial site views, but also the Scramble Experience, an audio-visual exhibition bringing to life what it was like for those who fought and supported the battle. Altogether a memorable few hours can be spent here, and out of season the atmosphere of the site is, to my mind, even more keenly felt.

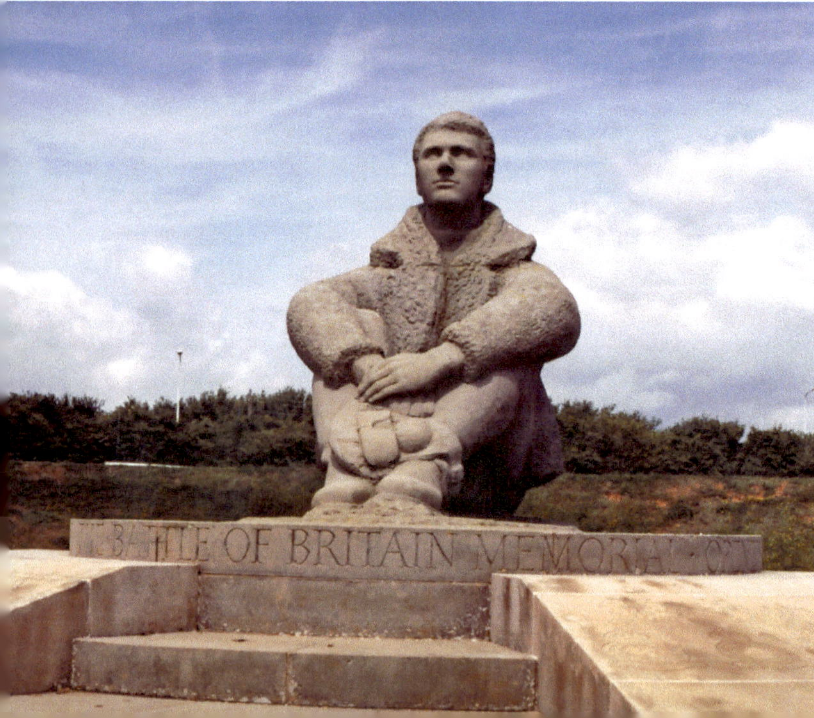

Battle of Britain Memorial statue, Capel-le-Ferne.

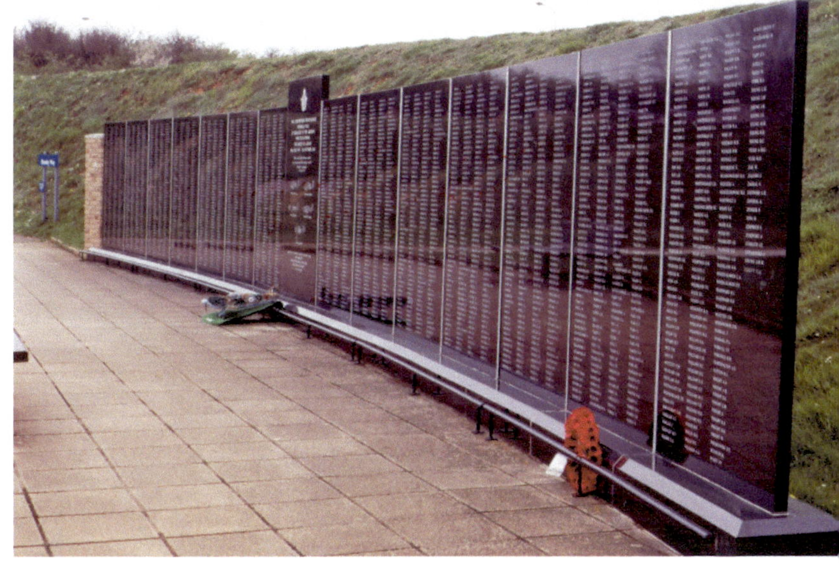

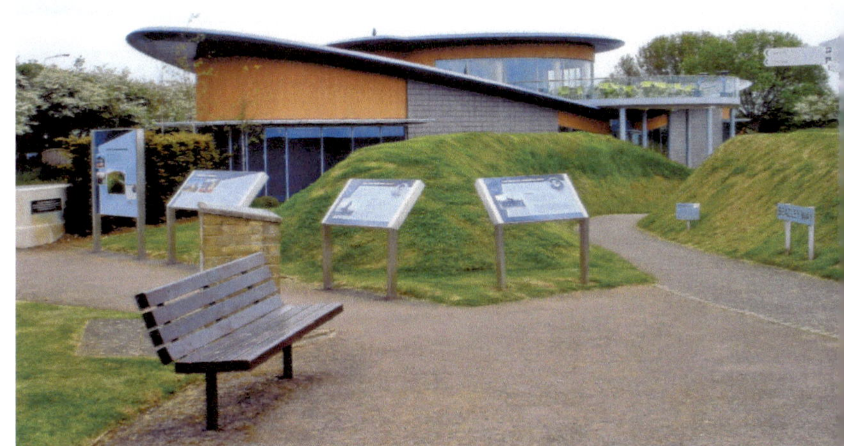

18. Samphire Hoe

Often described as the 'newest part of Kent', Samphire Hoe is an expanse of undercliff grassland beneath the cliffs just west of Dover. This was created by nearly 5 million cubic metres of chalk marl, excavated during the construction of the Channel Tunnel and being dumped here to create this landscaped platform by the sea. Subsequently this was sown with appropriate seed and left to go wild. That was back in the 1990s; now, at the time of writing (2018) the area is a pleasant, hillocky grassland that plays host to skylarks, dragonflies, common blue butterflies and early spider orchids among many other species. Humans also come here in large numbers too and all the usual facilities are on hand to accommodate them. People come here to do a spot of angling, learn about the place from the Education Shelter and interesting information boards, but mostly to enjoy a walk by the sea beneath the high chalk cliffs. The walks are gently undulating, largely tarmacked and considered accessible for wheelchair users too.

The name 'Samphire Hoe' originated from a competition organised by Channel Tunnel operators Eurotunnel in 1994 to replace their label for the site, the rather functional 'Lower Shakespeare Cliff Site'. From the hundreds of entries received the judges chose Mrs Gillian Janaway's entry 'Samphire Hoe'. This is a reference to the rock samphire that grows here and was mentioned by William Shakespeare in *King Lear* when referring to those climbing on the cliffs gathering this plant in the vicinity. A cliff just east of Samphire Hoe and visible from it is named Shakespeare Cliff because of this connection.

To the west of Samphire Hoe the open grassland gives way to a shingle and rock beach where fossil sea urchins and glittering iron pyrites and marcasites can sometimes be found. There are also a couple of huts built on the no man's land immediately beneath the cliffs. There used to be a string of these shacks along this coast, with some people living here all year round. An information board near the car park here tells the whole fascinating story.

On Samphire Hoe.

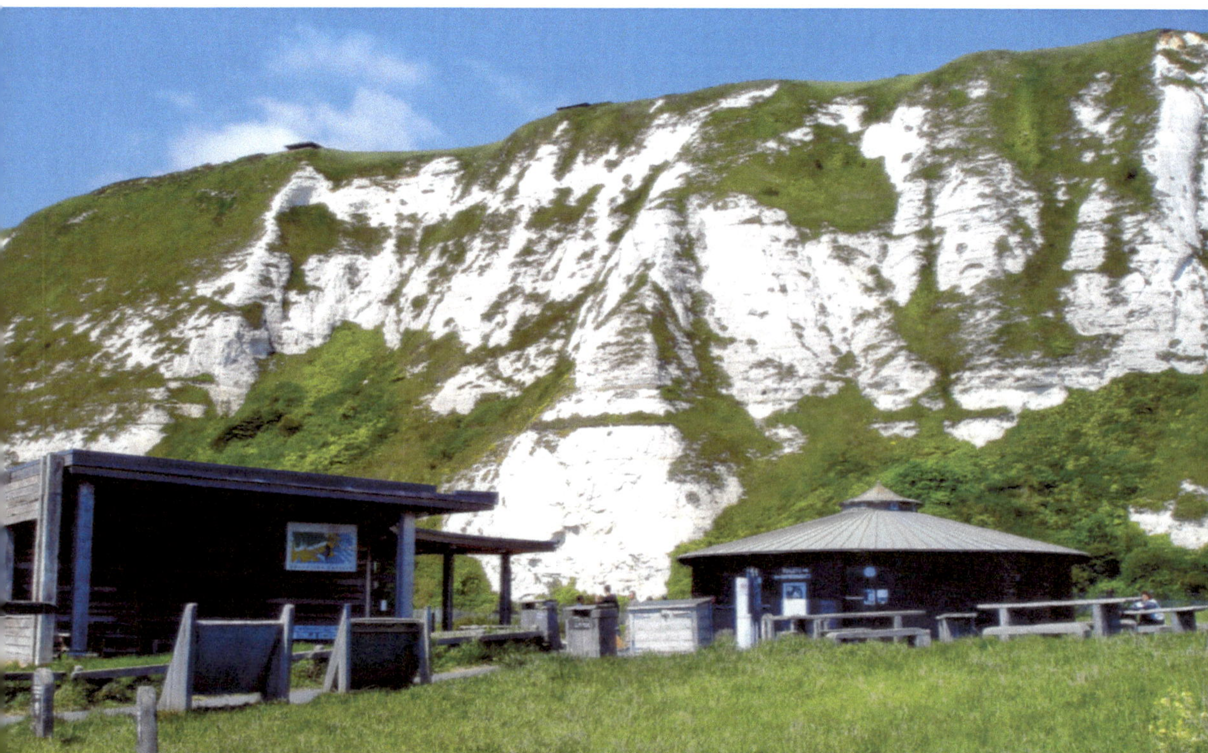

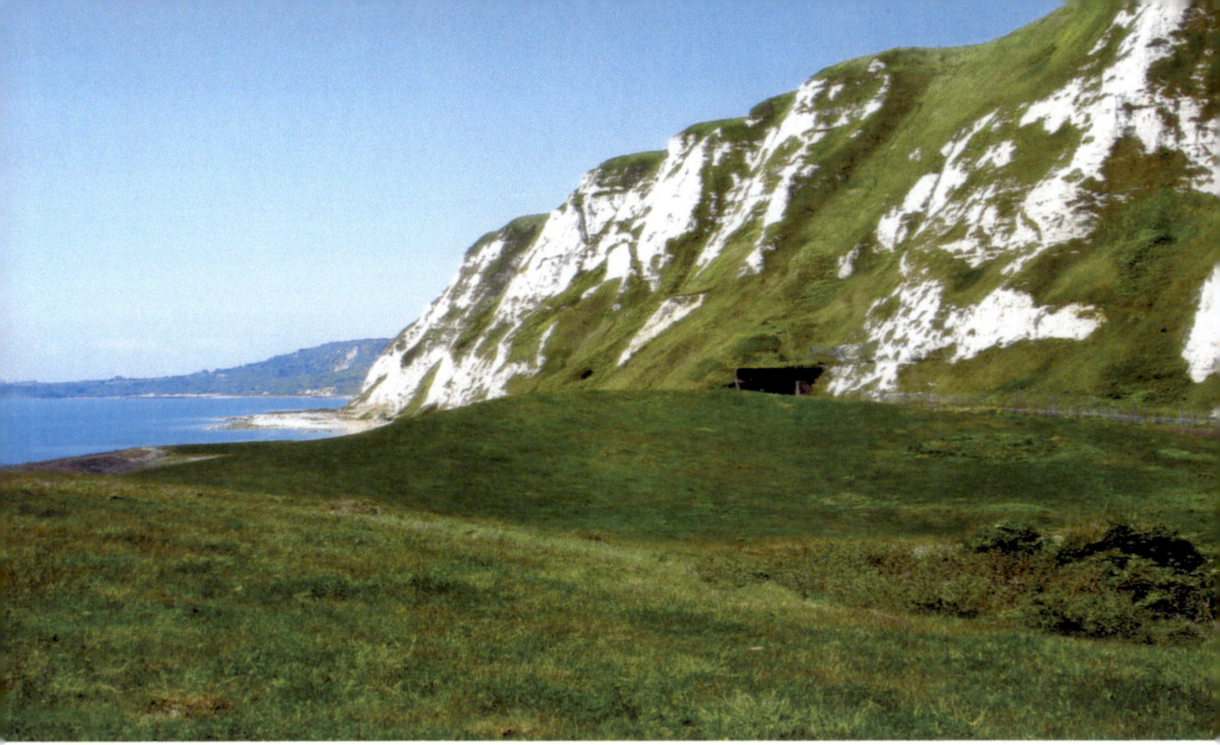

19. Dover Museum

In my childhood Dover Museum was in a different building and the poky entrance to it was guarded by a huge stuffed polar bear. Now the town's museum is in the light and airy modern Discovery Centre in Market Square, a building that also houses a tourist information centre and public library.

Dover Museum is a 'gem' to my mind because of its extensive, interesting and quite traditional layout with plenty of artefacts and reconstructions over its three floors. On the ground floor Dover's history from the Stone Age to the Saxon period is covered. The middle floor has special exhibitions; when I last visited in June 2018 it was the Zeebrugge Raid of 1918 that was featured. The top floor contains six scale models showing the growth of Dover from medieval times to the present day and good life-sized reconstructions of the inside of a Tudor house and the defence of Dover during the Napoleonic Wars.

Adjacent to the top floor is the state-of-the-art Bronze Age Boat Gallery, which contains the actual boat in a large display case, carefully preserved with surrounding exhibits relating to the boat and the Bronze Age itself, locally and in a wider context. There is a very good life-sized reconstruction of a Bronze Age hut and plenty of artefacts from those early times. For the record, the Bronze

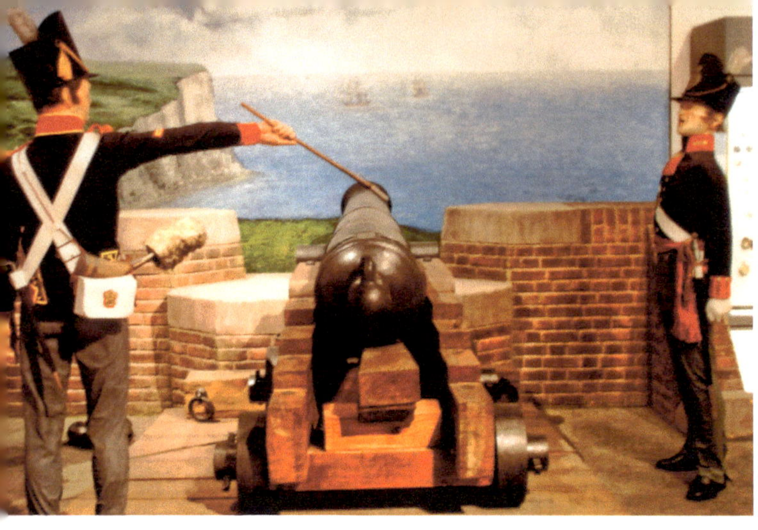

Scale model of soldiers defending Dover, *c.* 1812.

Age boat was discovered in 1992 in Langdon Bay, just east of the town. It had apparently foundered *c.* 3,550 years ago while carrying a cargo of 350 axes, daggers, chisels and other tools – many in bronze.

A short distance from the museum and linked to it by a path is the Roman Painted House, discovered in 1970 by the Kent Archaeological Rescue Unit. This is a fine example of a Roman house, complete with mosaics and underfloor heating. It was built in around AD 200 as a hotel for visiting traders, but was filled in and covered over in around AD 270 in order to build a fort. It was this infilling that preserved it over the centuries until its rediscovery. Opening hours are more limited than for the museum, which is open most days and is free.

As for the polar bear, it is still there and still surprising visitors by its sheer bulk but no longer in the entrance, having been consigned to the stairwell.

20. Kearsney Parks/Dour Valley

The River Dour emerges from the Kent Downs at the eastern end of the Alkham Valley. A beautifully clear, spring-fed chalk stream, the Dour descends through a series of lakes and small waterfalls as it tumbles its way for 4 miles down to the sea at Dover.

In its upper reaches the Dour has been utilised in a series of beautiful gardens. First Bushey Ruff, where there is a large lake surrounded by woods and footpaths. Next we come to Russell Gardens, which is in a formal style, and finally to Kearsney Abbey gardens, beautifully landscaped and with ample car parking and facilities.

Russell Gardens is Grade II listed by English Heritage and has as its centrepiece a canal pond crossed by Palladian-style pergola bridges through which miniature waterfalls tumble.

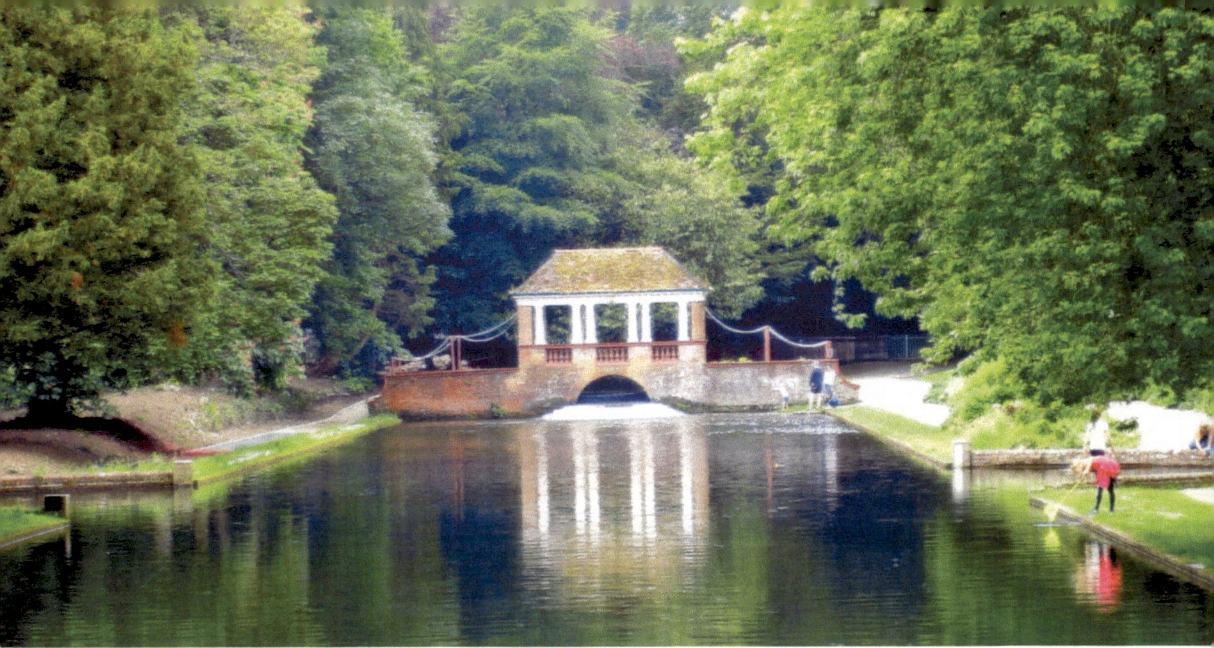

Across the road is the popular parkland expanse known as Kearsney Abbey after a large mansion house (never an abbey) that once stood here. All that is now left is the magnificent billiard room, now used as a café. The grounds are well landscaped around an ornamental lake and fountain, and much frequented by a variety of waterfowl that can show a marked interest in your sandwiches! There are fine tree specimens here, including beech, lime, yew and, most prominent of all, a huge cedar of Lebanon, said to be one of the oldest examples in the country (though at the time of writing roped off for safety reasons).

Walking south, out of the Kearsney Abbey park, brings you through a sun-dappled woodland criss-crossed with streams that combine to tumble into waterfalls through the ruins of the old River paper mill (not the old abbey as I believed as a teenager).

The River Dour was at one time instrumental in turning the wheels of thirteen mills along its length – mostly corn or paper mills. Slightly further downstream from Kearsney, just beyond another beautiful lake, stands the only one of those still operating – the Crabble Corn Mill.

This is said to be the most complete working example of a Georgian watermill in Europe. Built in 1812 on a site that would have been milling since the eleventh century, it operated until 1893. In 1990, after refurbishment, the mill was opened as a tourist attraction and makes a fascinating visit. Flour is produced here using the original milling stones and one can wander its floors and see it all happening.

Following the stream into Dover, we pass the site of Buckland corn mill, which in an earlier and lost incarnation was operating way back in the year 762 (the earliest documented in Britain apparently). The Dour passes through Dover's parkland at Pencester and enters the sea at Dover Harbour. The whole route is now the Dour Valley Walk, a trail laid out by the White Cliffs Countryside Partnership.

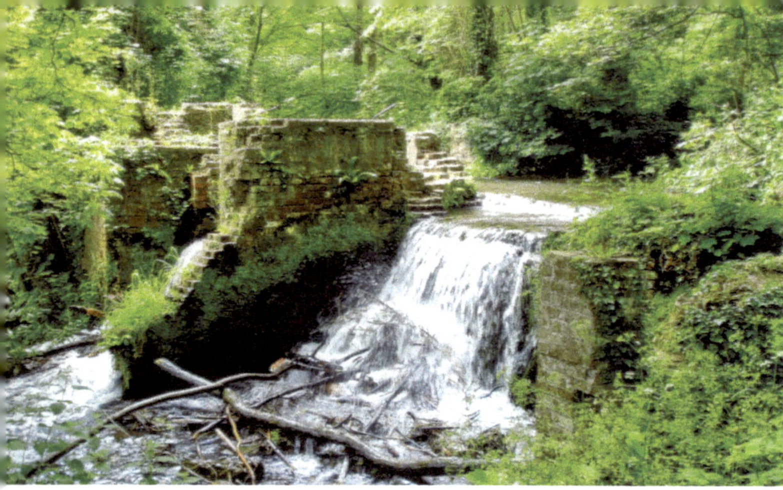

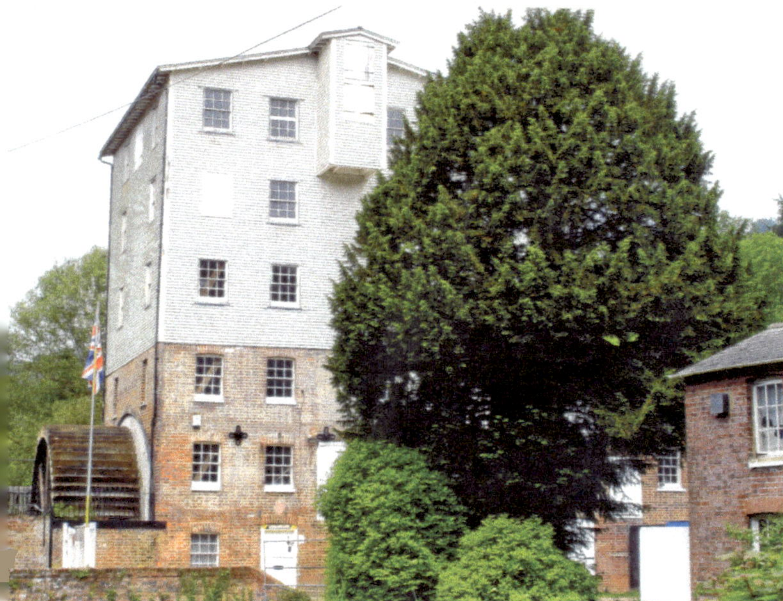

21. Dover Castle

Standing majestically above the town and visible for miles around, Dover Castle cannot fail to impress. Once known as the 'key to England', Dover Castle was mostly built in the 1170s during the reign of Henry II, although there was an earlier Norman earthwork here and a Saxon church, and the remains of a Roman pharos (lighthouse) can still be seen today. The castle covers a vast area and was the first concentric medieval fortification built in this country. It has two main entrances today, some way apart – one for vehicles and another through the Constable's Tower for pedestrians.

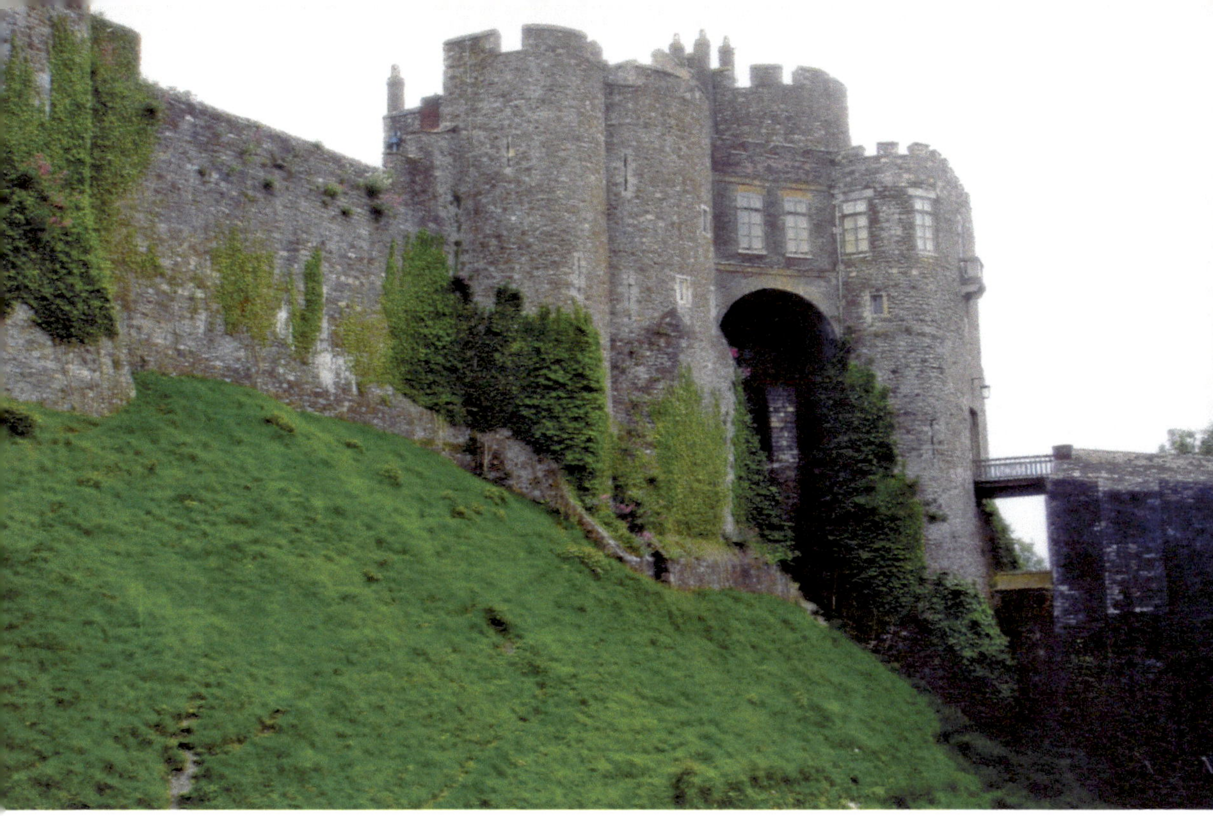

You can easily spend a whole day here; in fact, to do the castle justice this is what you would need. My favourite aspect is the keep, also known as the Great Tower. Walking around this sturdy and atmospheric building is a revelation. The many rooms of the keep were not the empty grey stone chambers generally imagined but colourful, luxurious apartments fit for a king. The King's Hall is dominated by a canopied throne, decked with wall hangings and housing recreations of contemporary furniture. Costumed actors playing the parts of Henry II, his queen and family hold court in some of the rooms and wander the keep and surrounding grounds telling their stories to the many thousands of visitors from all over the world who explore this medieval wonder almost every day of the year.

Around the castle and its grounds the various phases of its history can be explored, and to some extent experienced. The siege of Dover Castle in 1216, its use in both world wars (particularly as the headquarters for Operation Dynamo, which in 1940 mobilised a navy of small boats and ships that sailed to France to evacuate British and French troops from the beaches of Dunkirk), and secret tunnels to be used as a potential regional seat of government in the event of a nuclear war are all represented, and more.

There are also many events, re-enactments, mock battles, archery, costumed characters and projected figures explaining themselves and even spooky ghost walks, all in a setting better than any film set. If you like castles, they don't come any better than this!

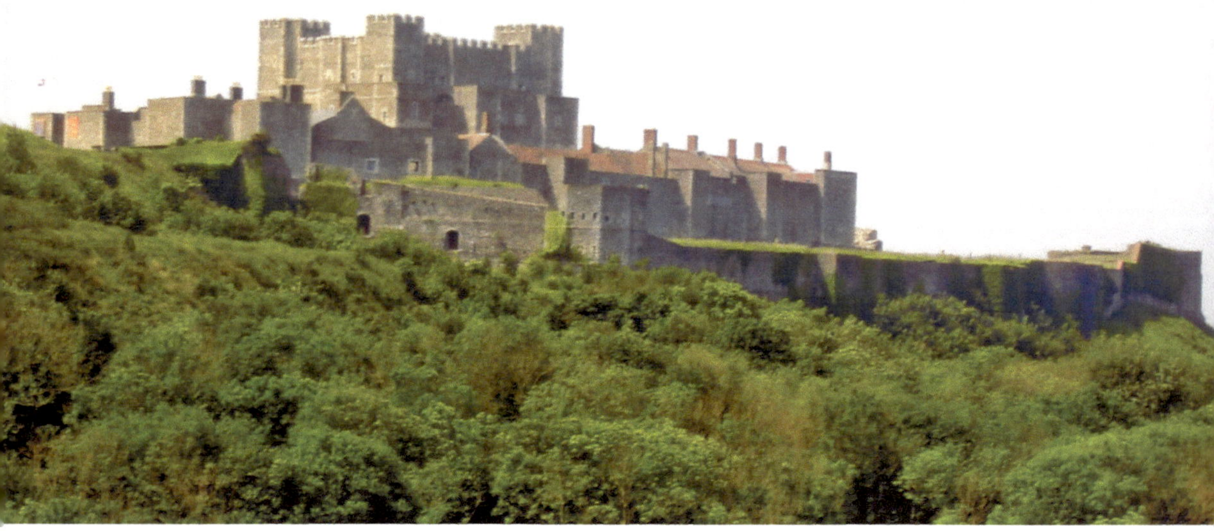

22. Langdon Cliffs

Despite stretching from Folkestone to Kingsdown, the 'White Cliffs of Dover' are usually thought of specifically as those stretching from Dover to South Foreland. Much of this is National Trust land and includes a large visitor centre with plenty of car parking at Langdon Cliffs above Dover's busy Eastern Docks.

This is a most pleasant stretch of cliffs where you will find open downland gently undulating atop gleaming white sheer cliffs that drop straight down to the rocky shore below. These are the classic white cliffs of the famous wartime Vera Lynn song. Exmoor ponies wander amiably about while skylarks (not bluebirds) twitter overhead. The rich National Trust-managed grassland is alive with bees and butterflies during the summer months, the latter including the rare chalkhill blue and the beautiful adonis blue. The landscape seems devoid of litter, while the straight level footpaths allow a good two or three hours of fine walking. In August 2013, the National Trust published a list of their top ten lesser-known recommended walks. The White Cliffs of Dover was in the number one position. I was walking the route just two days later and I think I could, at the time, safely say it was not a secret anymore!

If you don't fancy walking all the way to Kingsdown and perhaps have a car parked at the National Trust Visitor Centre that needs to be returned to, you might prefer a shorter wander along to the South Foreland Lighthouse and back. This is still a good walk with good views but perhaps a more practical length for many. This lighthouse, gleaming white, is the highest located of any in Britain – being 300 feet up on the clifftop. It is also the first place in Britain to catch the sunrise on New Year's Day, so I am told. It's historical claim to fame is that it was here that Marconi carried out the first successful ship to shore radio transmissions back in 1898 and the first cross-Channel radio transmissions the following year. There are guided tours most summer afternoons and teas for the weary.

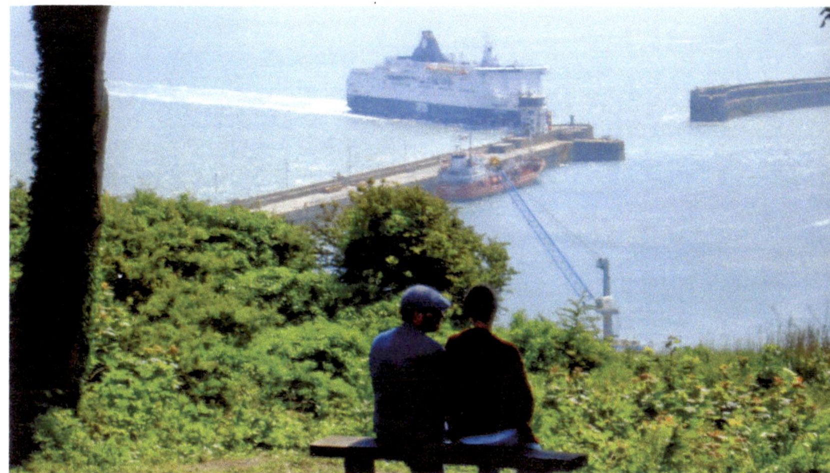

Above Dover's Eastern Docks, Langdon Cliffs.

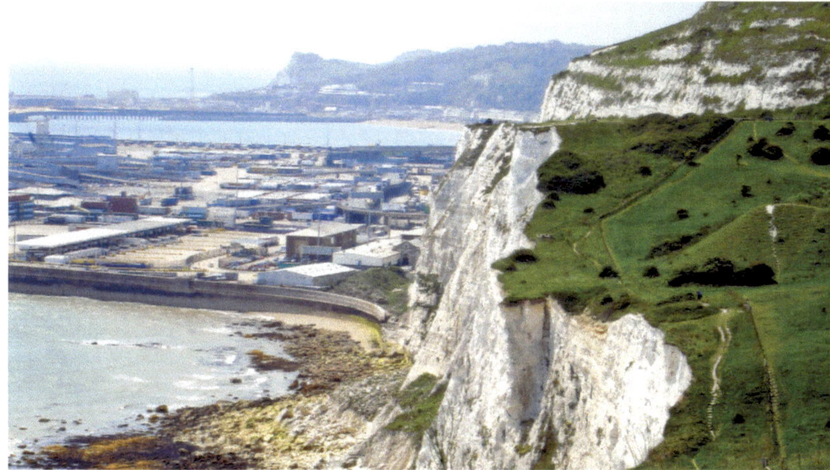

On the White Cliffs looking towards Dover.

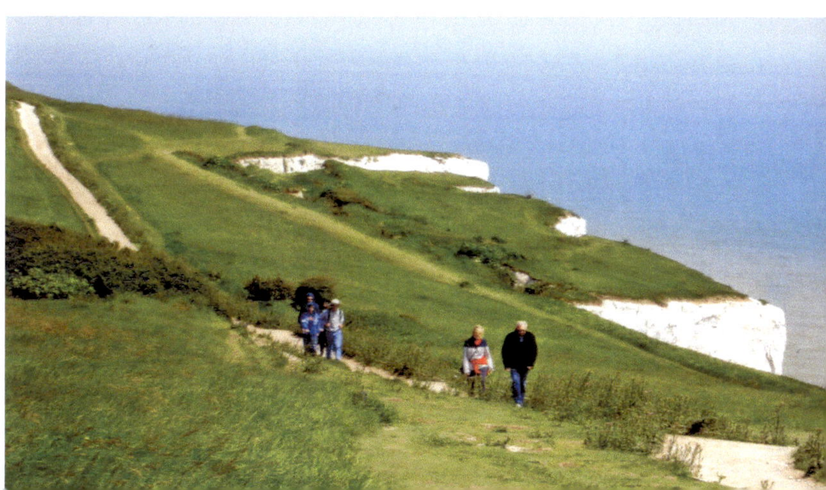

Walking the White Cliffs.

East Coast

23. St Margaret's Bay

This beautiful little bay marks both the point where England is nearest to France and also where the coastline changes from facing south-east to facing east. France is only 21 miles away, so consequently St Margaret's has become the starting point for many a Channel swimming attempt. There is also a very sheltered microclimate here, which has favoured an almost subtropical look to some of the gardens here.

A beautiful area of public gardens near the shore called the Pines is worth exploring. This contains a wealth of interesting plants, a grass labyrinth, cascade and an adjoining lake and a 9-foot-high bronze statue of Sir William Churchill, created by sculptor Oscar Nemon in 1972.

Right next to the sea, under the chalk cliffs is a large white house, once the home of playwright Noel Coward and later the novelist Ian Fleming, best known for his fictional spy hero James Bond. Fleming includes locations in East

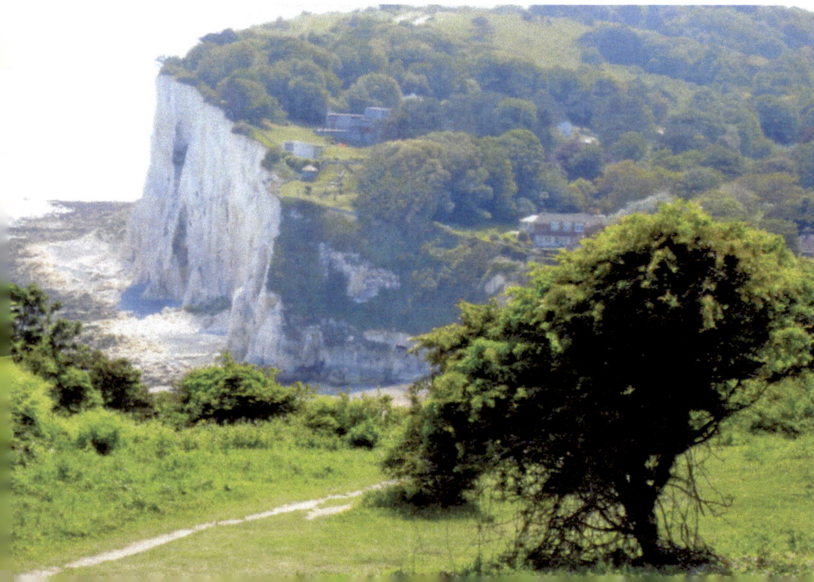

St Margaret's Bay.

Kent in a number of his tales, most especially *Moonraker*, published in 1955 – most of the story in this case being set around St Margaret's Bay and nearby Kingsdown. There was a film of *Moonraker* made in 1979, though it bore little resemblance to the original book and did not include local scenes at all – I recommend the book!

From the shore you can walk up a stepped path to the clifftop, where there are marvellous views, ponies grazing and a large Cleopatra's Needle-style obelisk. This was put up in 1922 to commemorate the work of the Dover Patrol in keeping the Channel shipping lanes open during the First World War. I often wonder if this great obelisk on the clifftop not far from Ian Fleming's house inspired his idea for the rocket base on these cliffs that featured in *Moonraker*.

Walking beyond the obelisk, with the sea on your right, brings you to what to me is the most pleasant walking stretch of the famous white cliffs. As the coast turns east facing, the quality of the air seems to change, becoming somehow calmer and less bracing, something I've noticed many times. The footpath is quieter too, with the number of walkers less than nearer to Dover. The cliffs are still gently undulating and fall like sheer white walls to the rocky beach below, but gradually lose height while a panorama of open countryside opens up ahead.

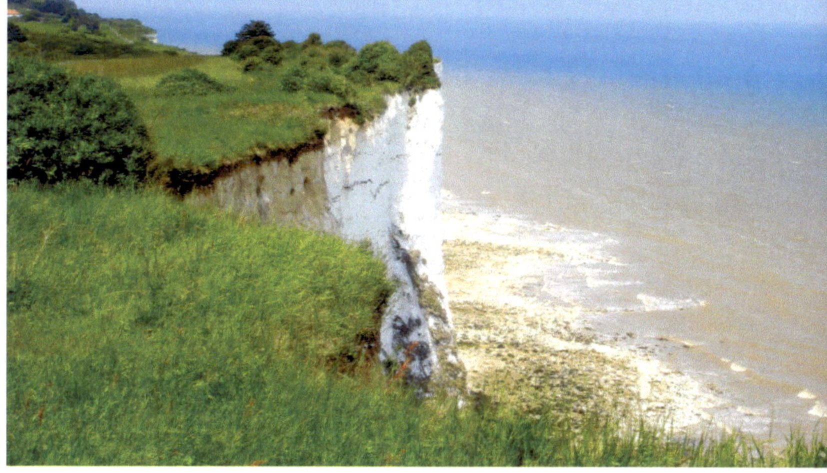

Cliffs north of St Margaret's Bay.

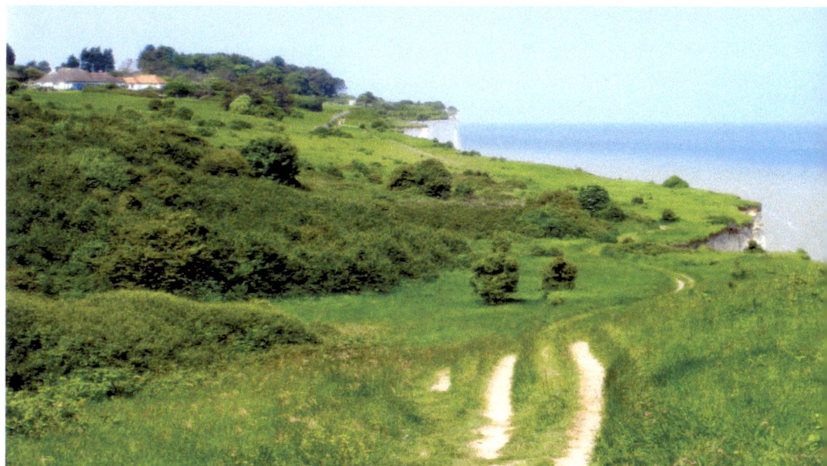

Towards Kingsdown.

24. Walmer Castle

At the end of the white cliffs, heading north, the resultant gap in the nation's natural coastal defences is immediately addressed by the presence of Walmer Castle. Or so thought Henry VIII, who had this constructed in 1538 along with several other similar castles from Camber in East Sussex through to Walmer, Deal and Sandown, with a view to defending the country against European forces supporting Rome against Henry in his disagreements with the Catholic Church. The invasion, like so many others, never came, but we are left with a distinctive string of castles, the best examples of which on the Kent coast are at Walmer and Deal. Seen from above, these castles reveal a series of concentric defensive walls that form the likeness of a Tudor rose.

Walmer Castle has, since 1708, been the official residence of the Lord Warden of the Cinque Ports, a medieval association of coastal ports in Kent and East Sussex. Some notable people have held this position, including Prime Minister William Pitt, the Duke of Wellington, Sir Winston Churchill and HRH Queen Elizabeth the Queen Mother. Today the post is occupied by Lord Admiral Michael Boyce.

The castle is open to the public and run by English Heritage. Today it has more the feel of a stately home than a military fortification, though there are still cannons on the walls pointing seaward. The interior of the building features elegant eighteenth-century panelling and numerous portraits and miscellaneous items relating to the Duke of Wellington. Behind the castle are 8 acres of fine gardens laid out to mark the ninety-fifth birthday of HRH Queen Elizabeth the Queen Mother. Various events are held in the castle and its grounds. I went along some years ago to a pleasant cream tea with music and entertainment on a theme relating to playwright Noel Coward.

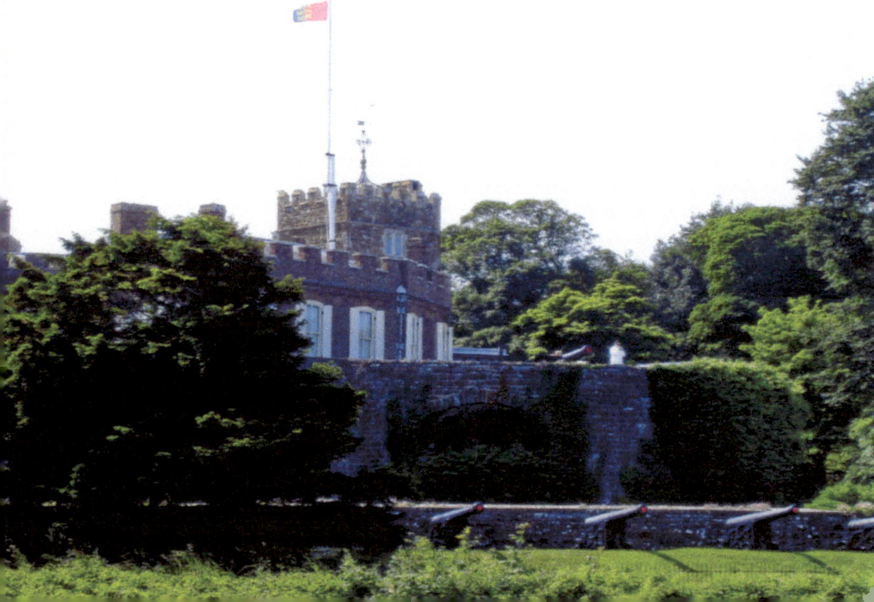

Walmer Castle.

25. Deal

There is something very nice about Deal, a feeling of cheerful, small-scale homeliness perhaps, a friendly, compact ambience, but then I may be biased. It was here that I spent much of my pre-school years and first attended primary school at the Deal Parochial. Then, it all seemed normal to me, nowadays the qualities of this pleasant little town are raved about as something special. Deal won the UK's Best High Street Award in 2014 and was recently named as one of the two best places to live in Kent. So what is it about this town that so appeals?

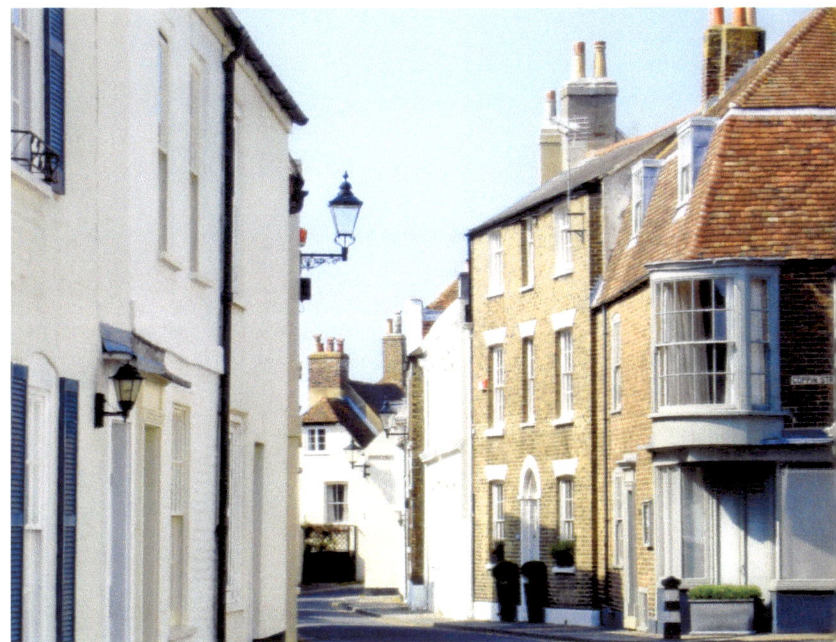

Middle Street, Deal.

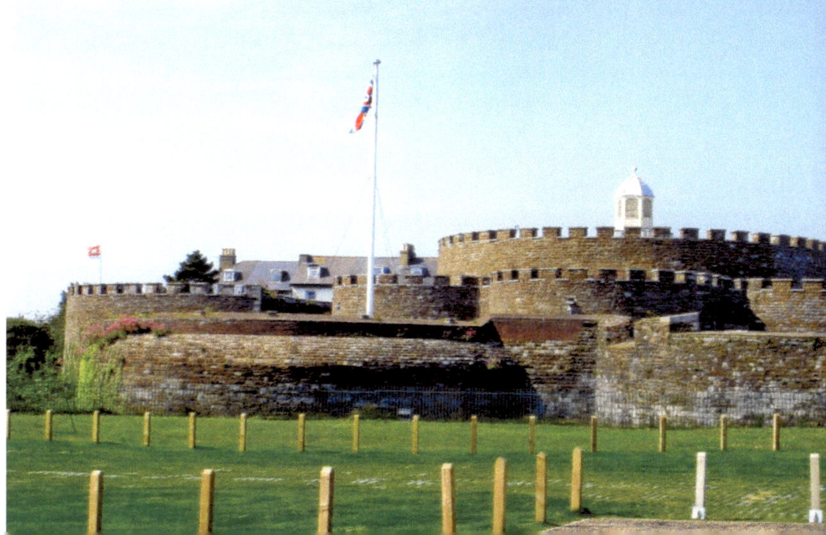

Deal Castle.

Maybe it is the Georgian architecture, the conservation area, the interesting houses and intriguing alleyways, the tales of smugglers, the bustling independent shops, fine eateries, friendly pubs, the tang of the sea or a combination of some or all of these.

I remember as a child the most fabulous fish 'n' chips from the Middle Street chippie, walks along the promenade with my parents to as far away as Walmer, Kingsdown and once all the way across the golf course to Sandwich Bay. We also regularly visited Walmer and Deal castles – the latter being the best preserved of Henry VIII's 'Tudor Rose' castles.

There is more, of course, that I have discovered as an adult – the museums, for instance. On the seafront is the Timeball Tower, where you can learn about this fascinating maritime aid that until 1927 used to signal to ships moored off or passing the town that it was 1 p.m. (as instructed from Greenwich) so that chronometers could be set. The Timeball Tower is operating again today for the benefit of visitors.

In St George's Road you will find the Deal Maritime and Local History Museum, where you can see a former Deal boat, the 'Saxon King', numerous artefacts and relics from the town's seaside history, the Deal Hooden Horse, a giant's shoe (!?), the history of the Royal Marines School of Music (whose fine former barrack building and memorial bandstand can be seen on the Walmer Strand) and much more.

A couple of streets away is the Museum of the Moving Image, historic Middle Street and South Street, where you can find the Queen Anne House, Carter House (former home of the famous scholar and 'bluestocking' Elizabeth Carter), the seafront promenade itself with the pier fronted by Jon Buck's fine sculpture – *Embracing the Sea* – and the Royal Hotel where Nelson used to meet Lady Hamilton.

So much of interest, so pleasant, I could go on all day.

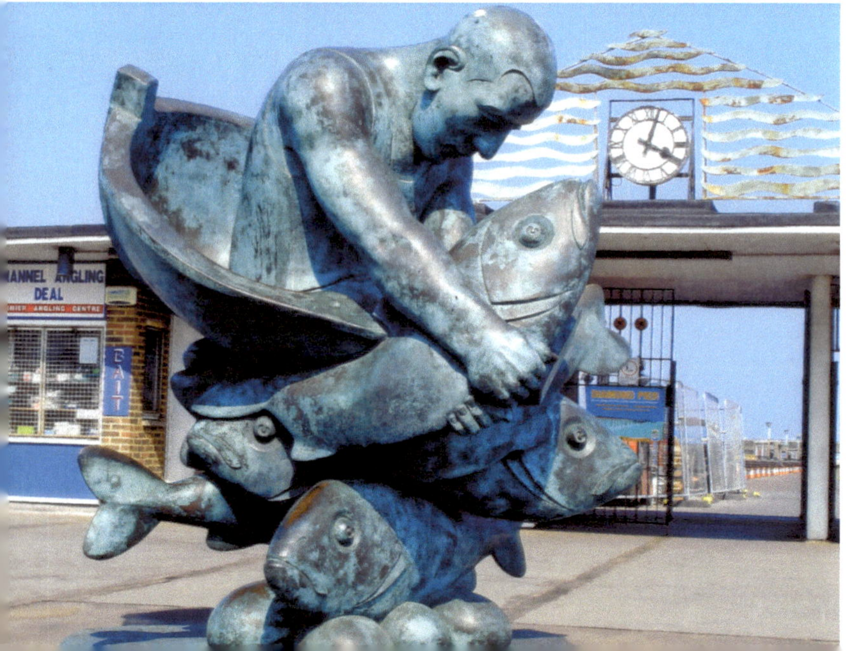

Jan Buck's sculpture *Embracing the Sea*, at Deal Pier.

26. Betteshanger Park

Just north of Deal, towards Sandwich, is a fascinating open space now known as Betteshanger Park. This area, of some 250 acres, is a raised plateau created from the spoil excavated by the mine workings of nearby Betteshanger colliery over many decades during the twentieth century. The Kent mines were closed down in the 1980s and the plateau-like spoil heap remained empty and unused for many years. It has slowly succumbed to nature as conifers, originally planted to stabilise the heap, spread, along with silver birch and latterly meadow grasses and flowers.

When the area was first being prepared to open to the public as a nature reserve in the early twenty-first century, I walked up there on several occasions and was captivated by this expanse of open, desolate landscape. The bare coal-dominated surface interspersed with areas of conifer and silver birch woodland, the surprising appearance of large numbers of the distinctive red with white spots fly agaric toadstools, and the bird haunted reed beds and marshland under a winter sky all conspired to remind me of my 1989 journey across Siberia. Such was its similarity that this became my 'Little Siberia', and for a while the scene of many walks.

By 2008 the plateau was open to the public and called Fowlmead Country Park, after the nearby Foulmead Farm. The area was developed for outdoor activity tourism and, along with nature's gradual colonisation of the plateau, changed its earlier desolate nature to something more welcoming and amenable. Now, what were empty expanses of coal spoil are covered in meadow grasses

Silver birch woodland, Betteshanger Park.

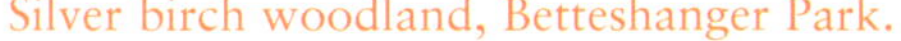

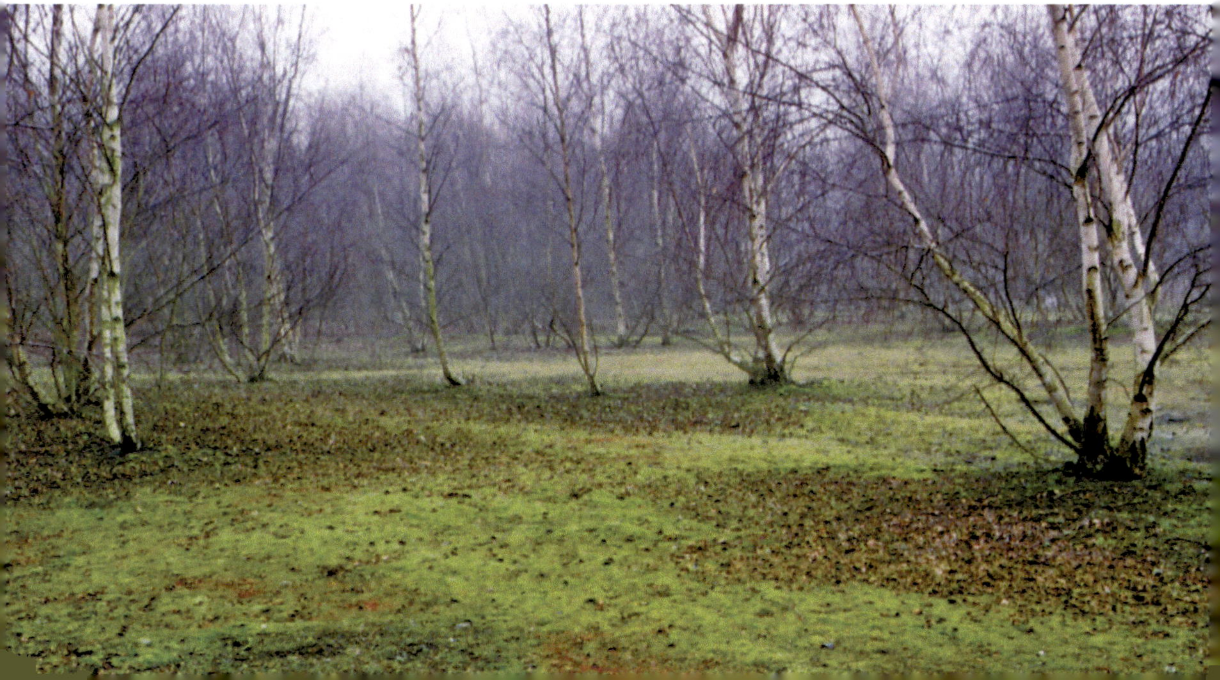

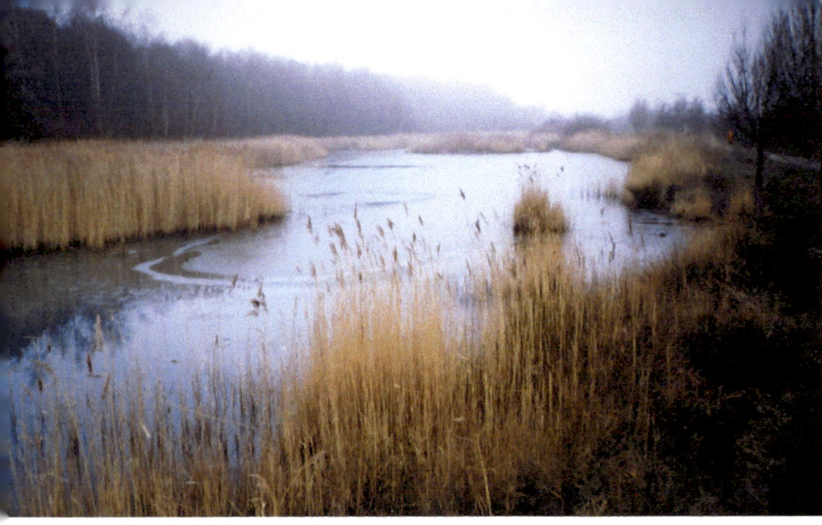

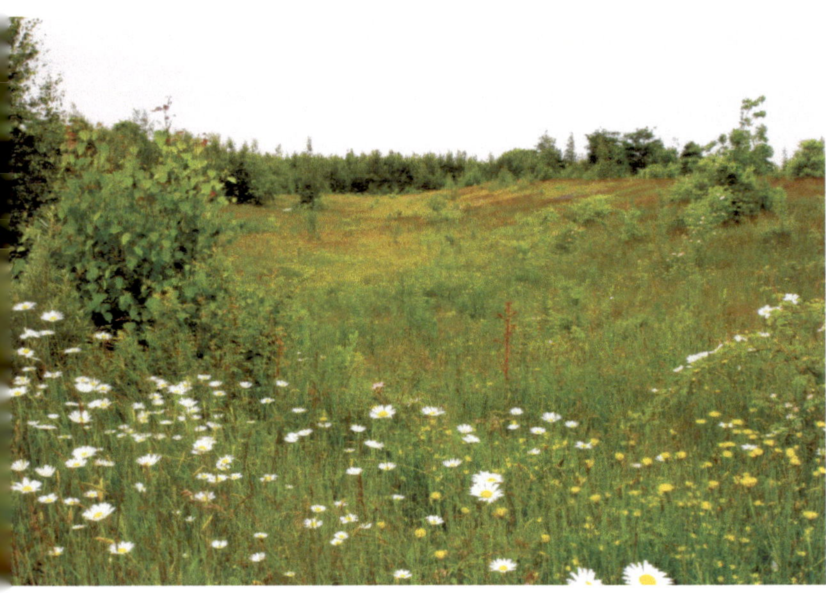

and ox-eye daises and visited by numerous butterflies and dragonflies. The ponds and lake are home to frogs, newts and water voles and play host to many migratory birds. Miles of cycle paths circle the park, now called Betteshanger Park. There are also mountain bike trails and fossil hunting sites as well as archery displays and tuition, military fitness training, walking routes and a state-of-the-art visitor centre.

A £40 million regeneration project has resulted in the opening of the Kent Mining Museum, a Green Energy Centre and the provision of a fleet of 100 bicycles for hire. The Betteshanger Sustainable Park project has been described as an 'economic and social regeneration project of national significance'. Indeed, an extremely good use of what had been an empty, post-industrial wasteland.

I think, though, for my next visit I'll go in the depths of winter or early spring and enjoy Betteshanger in its quieter season when I can again perhaps experience it as my 'Little Siberia'.

27. Sandwich

This wonderful little jewel of a town has been said to be 'the most complete medieval town in England'. Certainly it has nearly 400 listed buildings, from medieval to art deco, many of which can be seen from the top of St Peter's Church tower.

As you might expect, the place oozes history. The Guildhall (built in 1579), in the town centre, houses a museum that contains, among many other interesting artefacts and displays, a copy of the Magna Carta, only rediscovered in 2015. Wherever you look are medieval and Tudor buildings, such as those in Strand Street, which has more intact half-timbered buildings than any other street in England and is where the Flemish weavers set up shop.

The fourteenth-century town wall can be walked around for an overall view of Sandwich, which is attractive from any angle. Part of this is known as The

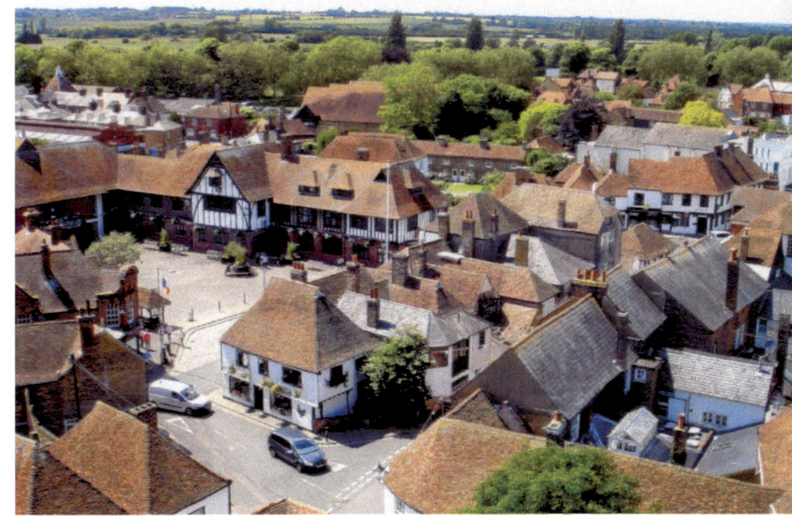

View over Sandwich from St Peter's Church.

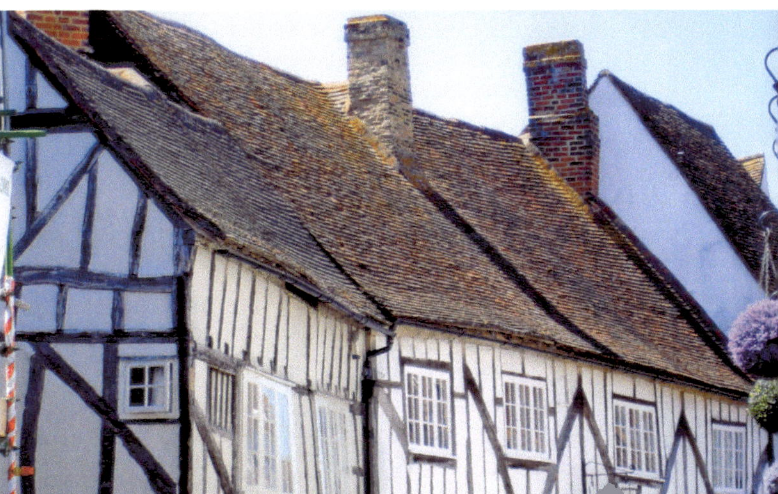

Strand Street, Sandwich.

Butts and is where Henvry V's archers practised before setting off to achieve their famous victory at Agincourt in 1415.

By the quayside the old toll bridge can be found, with its striking barbican building, much of which dates back to 1538 and includes even older stonework. Not far away is the one remaining town gate, known as the Fisher Gate, and nearby is Edwin Lutyens' Manor House, known as The Salutation, with its award-winning gardens. There is also a 1930s art deco cinema still in use near the market square; St Bartholomew's, one of the oldest established hostels for travellers and pilgrims, dating back to the 1190s; and the King's Lodging, dating to 1400, which is considered the finest period house in the town and where both Henry VIII and Elizabeth Istare are said to have stayed.

Outside the town can be found the White Mill Rural Heritage Centre, an eighteenth-century windmill with original wooden machinery, surrounded by a more extensive rural life museum with displays of farming interest, country crafts, wheelwrights etc. and a miller's cottage that was built in 1830, with two rooms set out as they would have been in the nineteenth century.

St Peter's Church, from where the fabulous views over Sandwich mentioned earlier can be seen, dates to the eleventh century and still rings a curfew bell at 8 p.m. (which I'm sure these days is just viewed as a quaint historical curiosity). Inside portraits of the various Earls of Sandwich can be seen, including John Montague, the 4th Earl. It was he who, one day in 1762, not wanting to come away from the gambling table to eat a meal, asked for two pieces of bread with meat in between – hence we have the 'sandwich'. This is apparently true and no apocryphal story – Sandwich really did introduce the sandwich to the world and, I suppose, therefore its similar successor the burger.

You may think of the burger as being an American speciality, so quite appropriately at St Peter's Church we have a link in that direction too, for it was here that one-time local resident Thomas Paine was married. It was Paine that wrote *The Rights of Man* and came up with a new name for the newly independent American colonies – the United States of America.

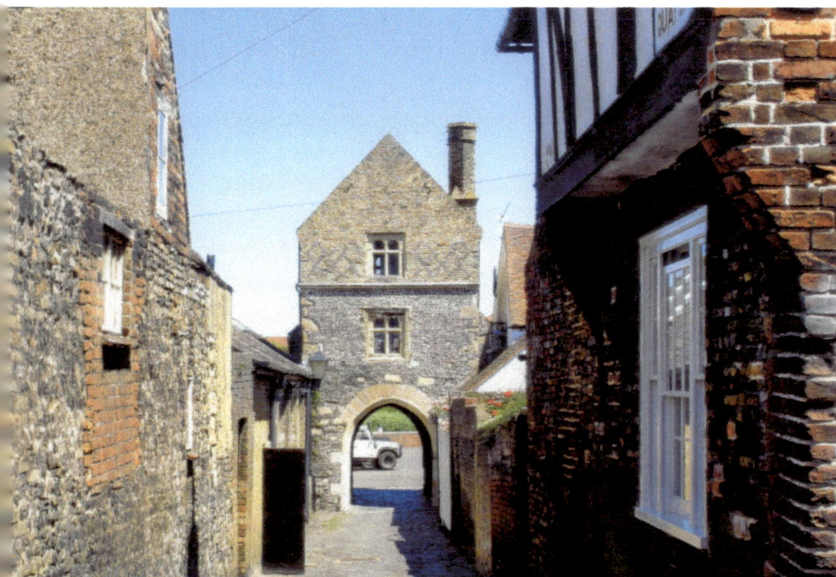

Fisher Gate, Sandwich.

28. Sandwich Riverbus

While in Sandwich and as an alternative to history, why not take a trip on the Sandwich Riverbus? A half-hour trip can take you around the town boundary, an hour upstream and back includes the Roman ruins at Richborough, but the trip I would recommend is the two-hour downstream and back excursion to where the River Stour meets the sea. Here, common seals are to be seen basking on mudbanks at the river mouth or swimming near the boat.

The river trips and seal-spotting excursions commence from near the toll bridge at times advertised by the blackboard (they vary according to the tides). I went on one and was delighted by this slow, low-tech chug up the river narrated by the boat's captain, who is none other than the Sandwich Harbour Master himself.

Although seal sightings are not guaranteed, there is a very good chance of seeing them. They are what are sometimes called harbour seals or more correctly common seals. They are cuter and smaller with rounder faces than the grey seals, which are much larger – up to 6 or 7 feet in length – with a longer snout and more dog-like face.

The Sandwich Riverbus only visits this colony of a couple of dozen common seals and not the 350 or so grey seals that are to be found on the Goodwin Sands out to sea. To view these you can take a high-speed boat trip out from Dover or Ramsgate.

Sandwich Riverbus can be contacted via their website(sandwichriverbus. co.uk) or by phone on 07958 376183.

Sandwich Riverbus.

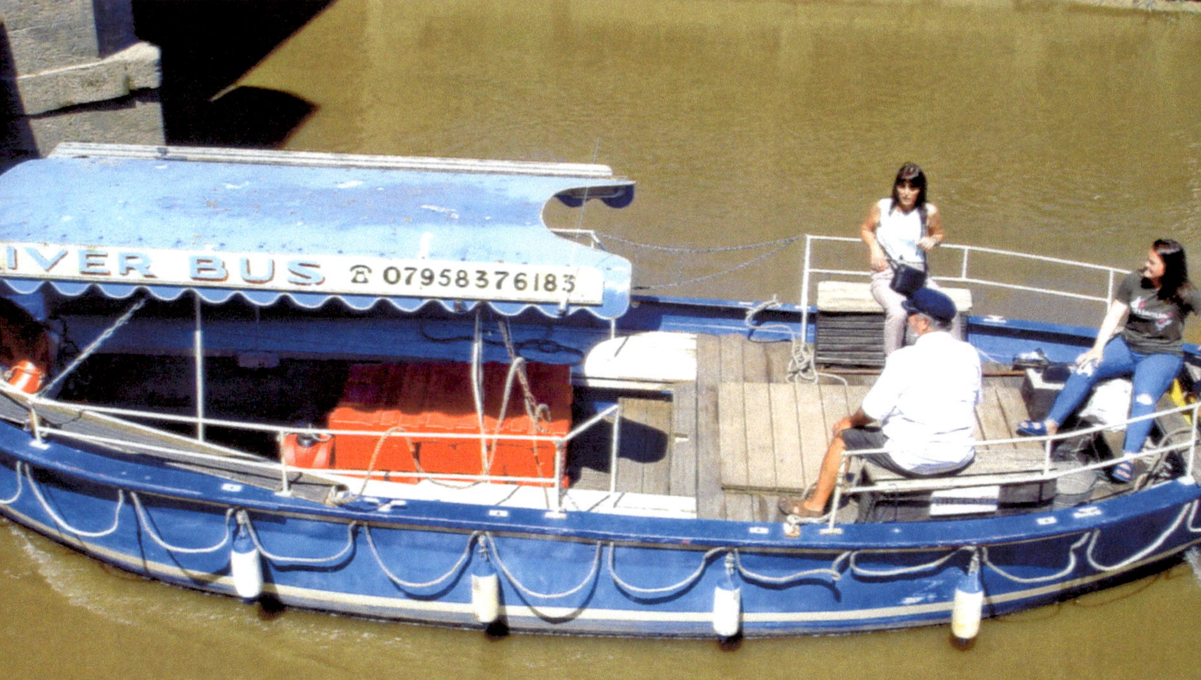

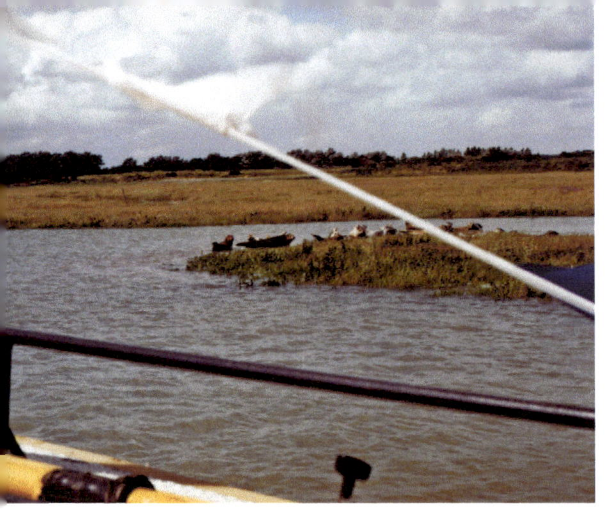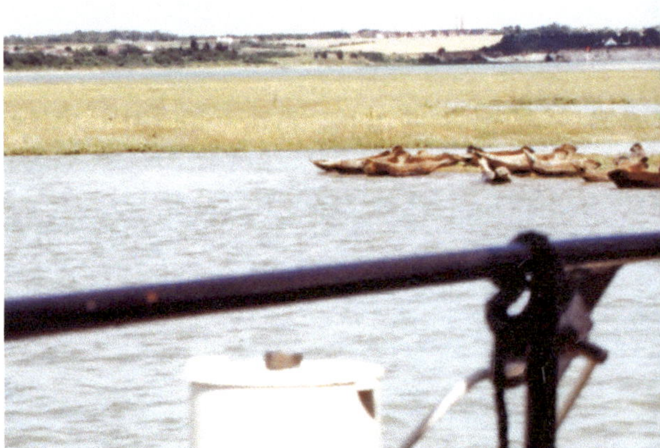

29. Richborough Roman Fort

Just upriver from Sandwich and accessible by Riverbus, as earlier mentioned, stand the imposing ruins of what is popularly known as 'Richborough Castle', more properly called Richborough Roman Fort, according to English Heritage, who run the site. A lot of research and excavation has been done here over the years, as you will find out when visiting. The fort was built in stages between the first and third centuries AD. The walls visible today date from around AD 270 – in common with the upgrading of other such forts around the country. This was probably in reaction to an increase in raids on the coastline by Saxons and Franks from across the sea, but also possibly a refortification *against* the Roman Empire by rebel British/Gallic commander Carausius, who created a breakaway faction of the empire for a short time. Imperial Rome did return, however, and retake the province of Brittania by the end of the third century.

Inside the fort the foundations of a monumental arch can be seen (one of the largest in the Roman Empire), along with an inn, town buildings, granaries, a shop, a bathhouse, a baptismal font and a Christian chapel. Outside the fort walls there is more evidence of a former town and port at the site, including a large amphitheatre that could seat an audience of up to 5,000. All this is difficult to appreciate from the walls and foundations alone, so recourse to the information boards, audio guides, on-site museum and guide books is recommended to fully understand the significance of what you see.

Although this was obviously once a bustling fort/town/port (particularly towards the end of the period of Roman occupation in the early fifth century (judging by the number of coins found from that period here) it has today a strangely calm ambience. Perhaps it is the quiet spot this now occupies next to the

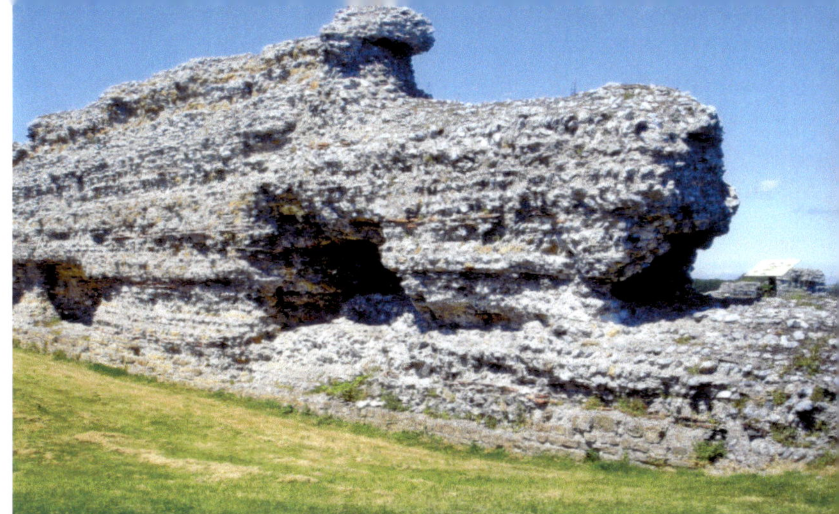

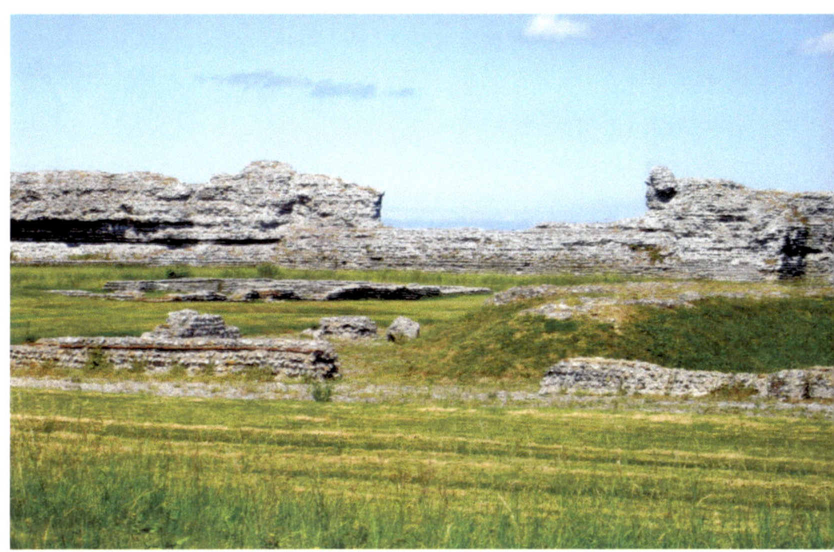

River Stour, but every time I go to Richborough I feel this unaccountable serene, secure, relaxed feeling. Maybe a distant, subliminal echo of what Richborough's inhabitants may have felt within the safety provided by these walls?

30. Cliffsend

Cliffsend is the small village at the southern termination of the white chalk cliffs of the Isle of Thanet where they are replaced by the reed beds and mudflats of Pegwell Bay. The attractive village sign sums up its main points of interest well: St Augustine's Cross (erected in 1884 to commemorate the landing of

St Augustine near here in AD 597), a SRN4 hovercraft (a reference to the hoverport operational here from 1969 to the 1980s) and at the top of the sign is the Viking Ship *Hugin*.

The *Hugin* is a replica of a Viking longboat of the ninth century given by Denmark to the Isle of Thanet to mark the 1,500-year anniversary of the landing of the brothers Hengist and Horsa on this coast in the year AD 449, an event that is said to mark the start of the subsequent Anglo-Saxon settlement of England. The longboat was built in Denmark (Hengist was said to be a dame) and rowed across the North Sea by a Danish crew to beach at Viking Bay, Broadstairs. From there it was brought to its current clifftop location at Cliffsend. In 2005 the ship was refurbished and seems to have been very well maintained since. The *Hugin* amazes by its size, I for one didn't realise how big and substantial Viking longships were.

The setting for the longship creates a pleasant stop for a cup of tea or snack and also serves as a picnic site. Walks lead down to the shore where the platform of the long defunct hoverport is still visible and south into the saltmarsh lands of Pegwell Bay with its abundant cord grass, food for the many wading birds that come here. Pegwell Bay is both a country park and a National Nature Reserve, along with nearby Sandwich Bay, on account of its migrating birds, eel grass, seals and sea holly.

There is also a path along the clifftop heading north that is probably safer than going in this direction at shore level, where there are apparently sometimes dangerous quicksands as well as the possibility of being cut off by the tide. There are caves cut into the cliffs with tunnels connecting to the clifftop that were used in the past by smugglers. One such tunnel connected with the Belle Vue Tavern where good Channel views have earned it the nickname 'the Balcony of Kent'. This pub was named Shepherd Neame pub of the year in 2017. A long-distance walk and cycle route called the Viking Coastal Trail can be joined at Cliffsend, which follows the old coastline of the Isle of Thanet (now landlocked on its western side).

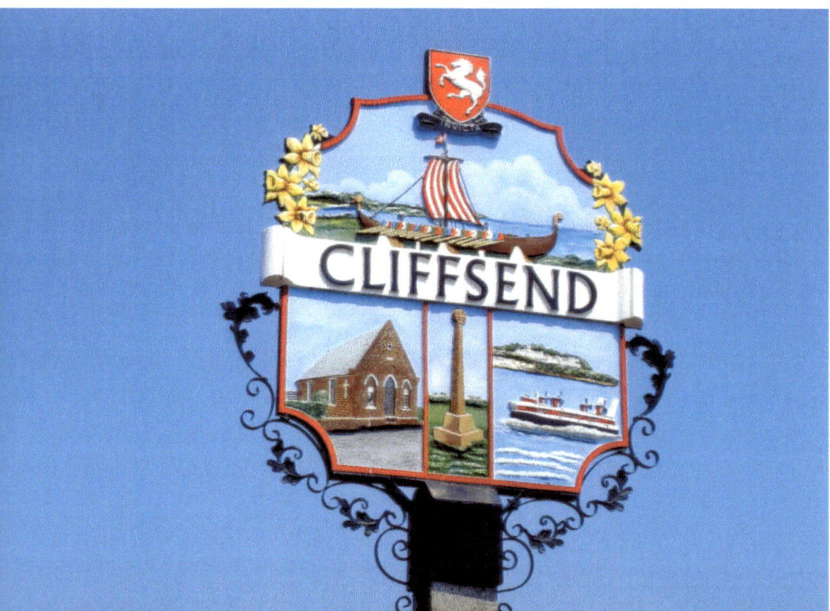

Village sign, Cliffsend, Pegwell Bay.

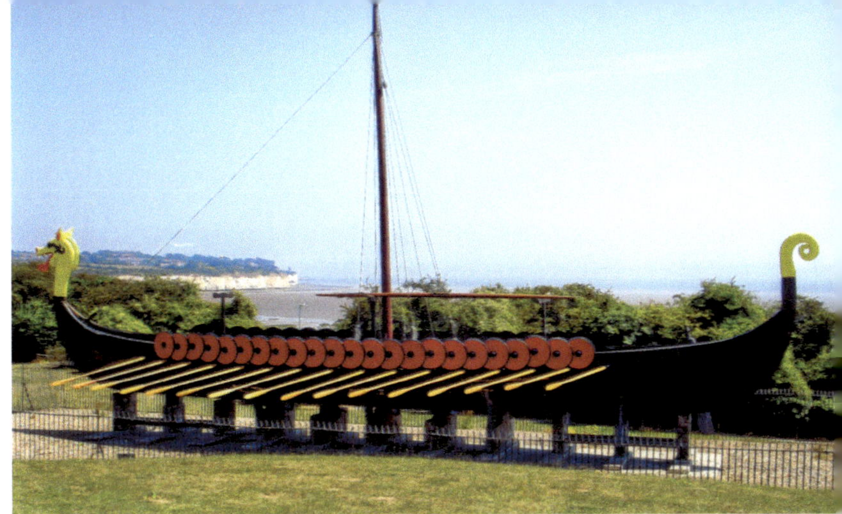

Viking ship *Hugin* at Cliffsend.

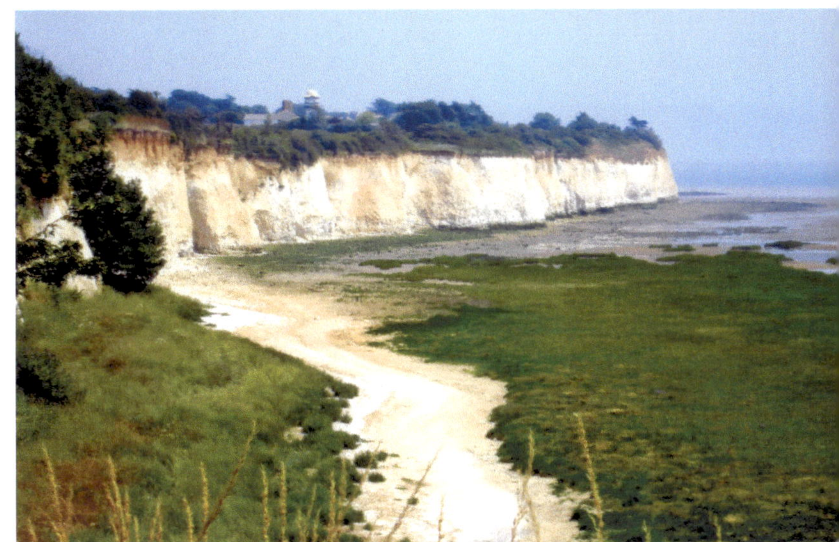

Coastline at Pegwell Bay, looking towards Ramsgate.

31. Spitfire & Hurricane Memorial Museum

Inland, to what at first seems the rather sad spectacle of the Manston airfield, the former Kent International Airport. Overgrown runways, an abandoned control tower and a vast expanse of very little create a depressing landscape. One day perhaps it might be fully utilised again, who knows? Meanwhile, there are at least two good reasons to come here: the Spitfire & Hurricane Memorial and RAF Manston History museums – both very interesting if you are into aviation, particularly of Second World War vintage.

The Spitfire & Hurricane Memorial has an example of each of the two iconic Battle of Britain fighters, fully restored and surrounded by numerous relevant artefacts and displays. There is also a recently installed Spitfire flight simulator, which was proving very popular with a party of elderly men when I last visited. A visit here compliments one to the Battle of Britain Memorial at Capel-le-Ferne mentioned earlier in this book.

Just across the car park, easily recognisable by the V-I 'doodlebug' flying bomb mounted outside its entrance, is the RAF Manston History Museum, which is full of aircraft or parts of them along with other exhibits telling the story of Manston airfield from 1916 up to the present day.

With a café and facilities on hand a good half-day out can be had here if aviation, particularly military, is your thing.

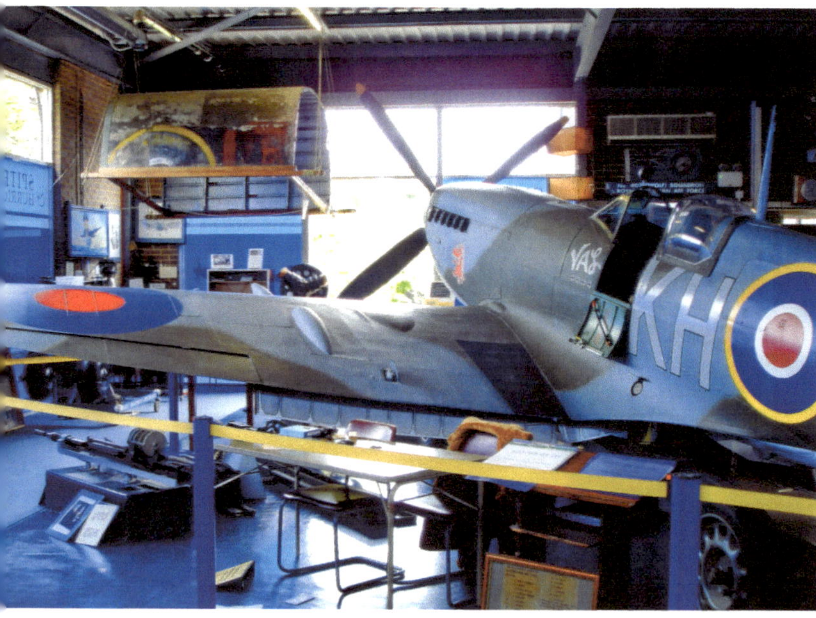

Spitfire on display at the Spitfire & Hurricane Memorial Museum.

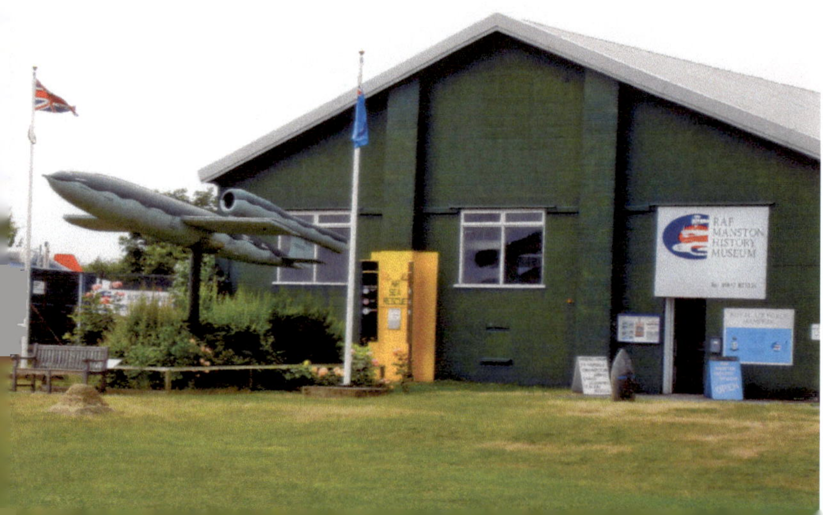

V-I displayed outside RAF Manston History Museum.

32. Broadstairs

Back on the coast, this delightful little town never fails to impress. On my most recent visit I found it neat, tidy, clean and with a sort of pleasant, low level, restrained, polite bustle. This is no brash seaside resort.

Broadstairs got its name from a flight of steps carved into the chalk cliff that led up to the medieval shrine of St Mary. At one time it was a smuggler's haven, but in the nineteenth century became an upmarket resort. Today its golden beaches, many bays, little pier and beach huts attract a steady stream of visitors, some drawn by its Charles Dickens connections.

Dickens spent summer holidays in Broadstairs during the 1850s and 1860s and there is a Dickens Museum containing letters and personal items of the great writer here, just back from the sandy Viking Bay. Up above the town on a high promontory at the north side of this bay, a large castellated building called Bleak House (a reference to the Dickens novel of the same name) can be seen. In case you were wondering, he didn't write *Bleak House* here. The house was originally called Fort House, for obvious reasons, and was given its current name because Dickens wrote *David Copperfield* while staying here on some of his regular visits. Today the building is a Grade II listed hotel and wedding venue but does do afternoon teas and I understand provides access to one of Dickens' study rooms. In the town itself there is the annual Dickens Festival.

Viking Bay, Broadstairs.

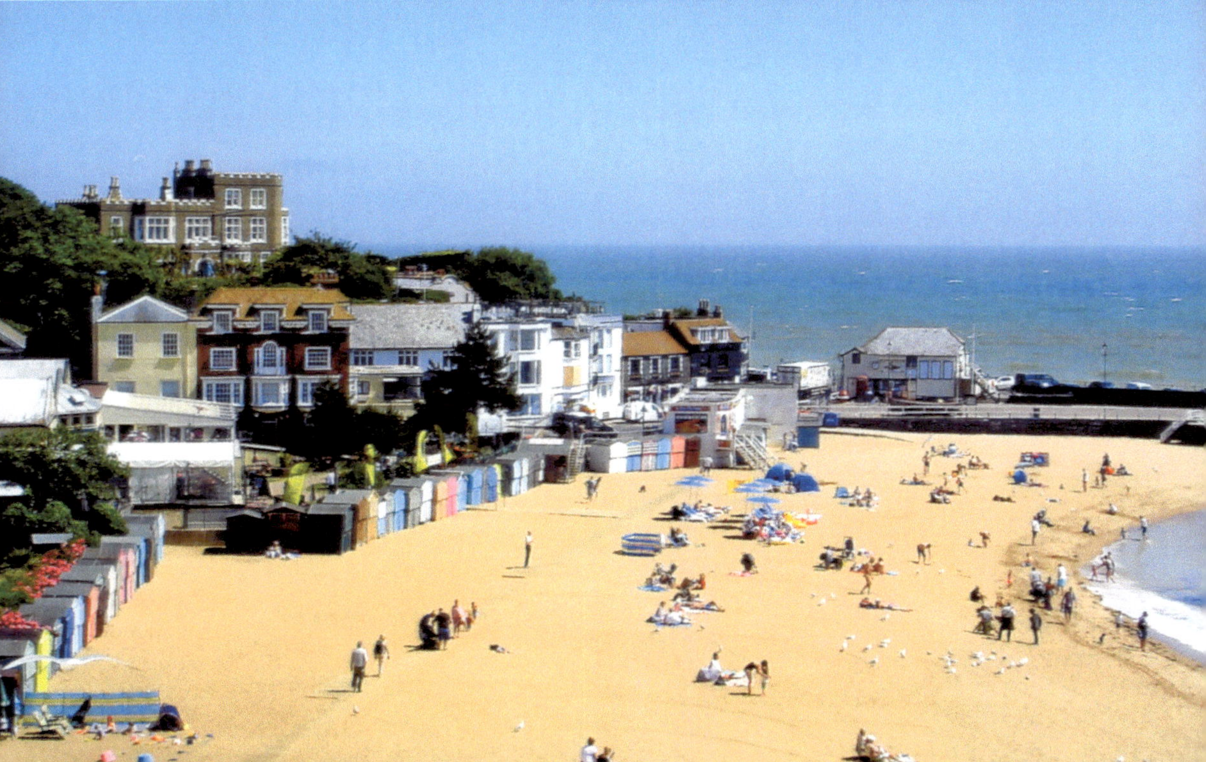

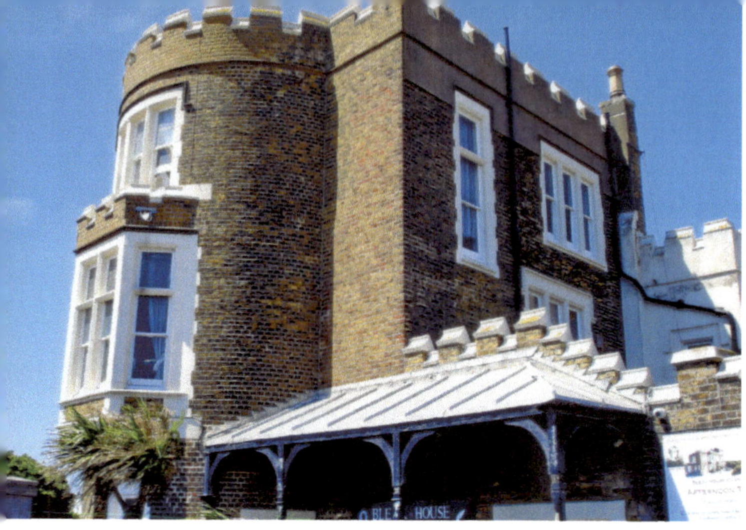

Bleak House, Broadstairs.

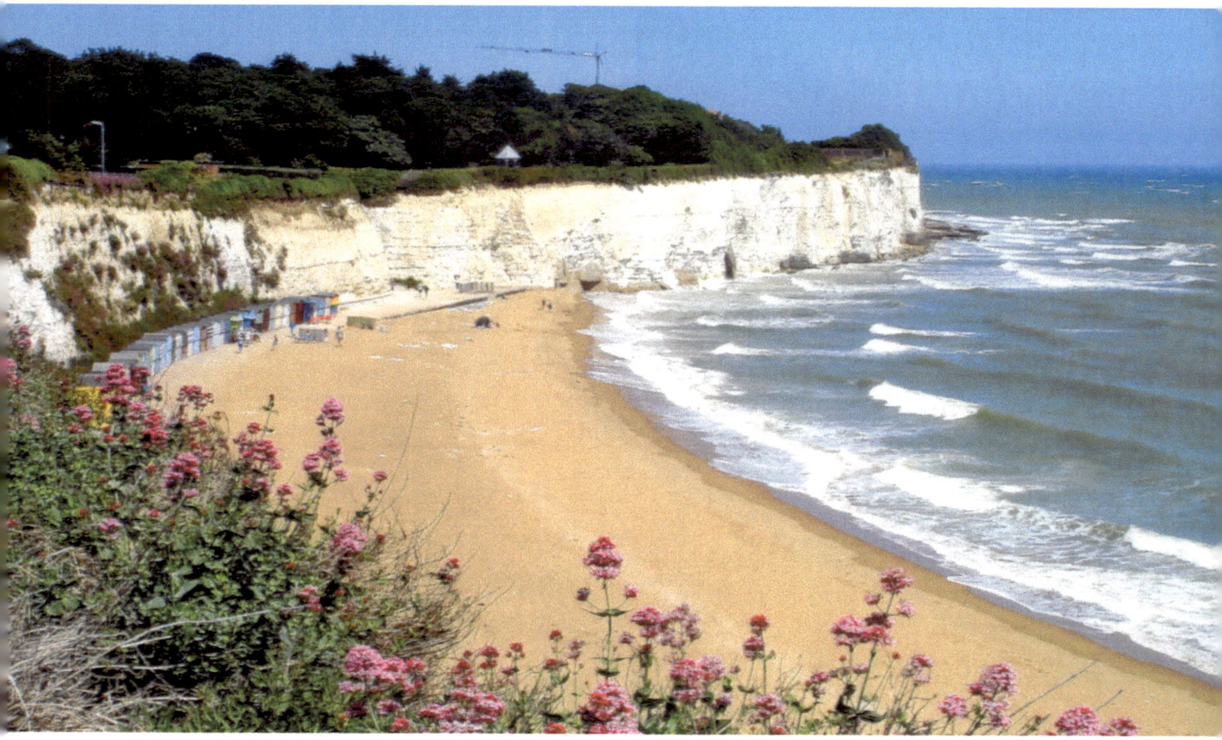

Stone Bay, Broadstairs.

A short distance north from Bleak House brings us to one of Broadstairs's sandy bays. Known as Stone Bay, this clean beach won the 2018 Blue Flag award and has an unfrequented feel about it, despite being not very far from the town. Another mile further on is Joss Bay, the best surfing beach around here apparently and sometimes heaving with people, no doubt assisted by the presence of a car and coach park next to it.

Broadstairs has something for everyone and few more relaxing and beautiful places are to be found on the Kent coast. This is definitely one of my favourite 'gems'.

33. Kingsgate Bay

Continuing north past the imposing, white North Foreland lighthouse brings you to the sheltered Kingsgate Bay, a sandy beach backed by chalk cliffs containing some fine sea caves and a sea cliff arch.

Taking the steps up from this fairly unfrequented beach brings you to the Captain Digby pub, which is housed in what appears to be a small castellated fort. Here you can drink or dine on the breezy chalk clifftop with views across the bay to Kingsgate Castle, which looks very medieval but was in fact built in 1860 for the 1st Baron Holland as a stable block then later converted into a private residence for Lord Avebury, the man who introduced bank holidays to Britain in 1871. More recently, the 'castle' has been divided into apartments.

The flight of seventy steps that lead down from the Captian Digby pub to the beach are thought to be the inspiration for the title of John Buchan's famous tale of espionage *The 39 Steps*, which he wrote while convalescing from a stomach ulcer on the North Foreland in 1915. Buchan changed the number of steps from seventy to thirty-nine for the title of the book. The story was later made into the now classic film by Alfred Hitchcock.

A short distance north of here, following the coastal footpath, brings you to another strange castle-like structure in ruins and with no indication as to its former purpose – curious. I looked it up on the Ordnance Survey map and

Cliffs, caves and sea arch, Kingsgate Bay.

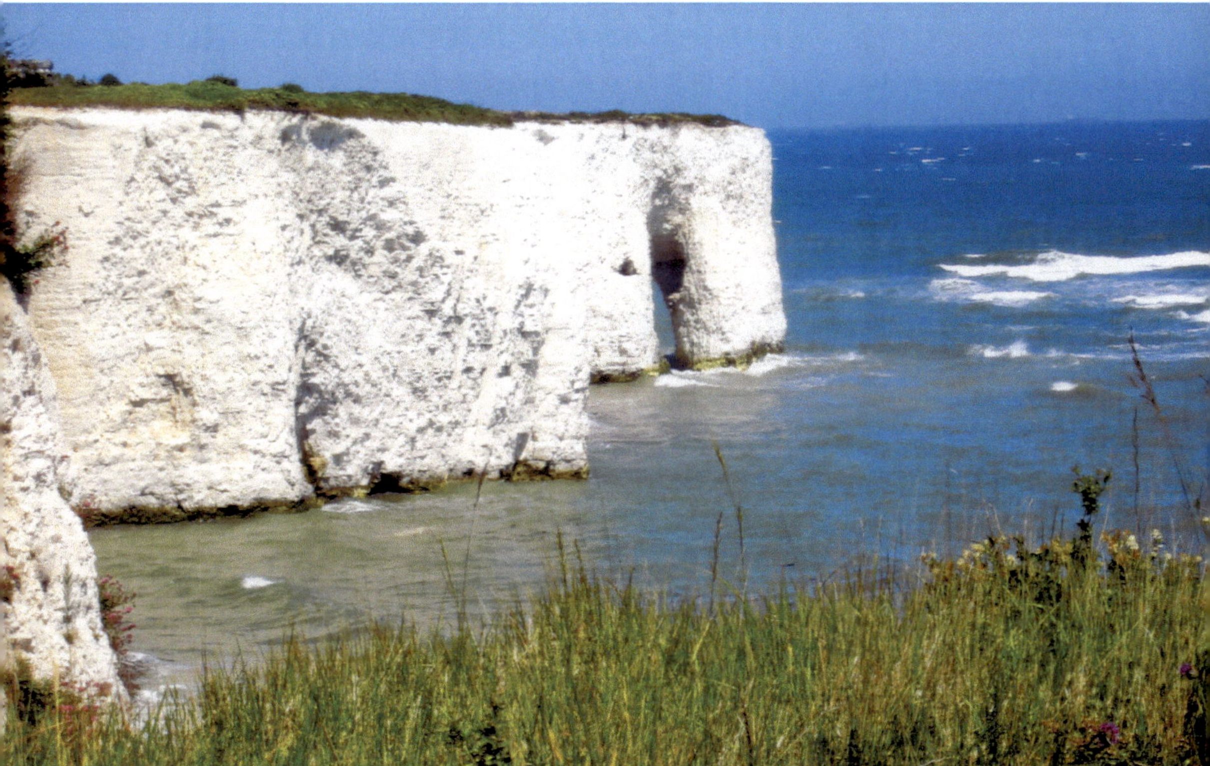

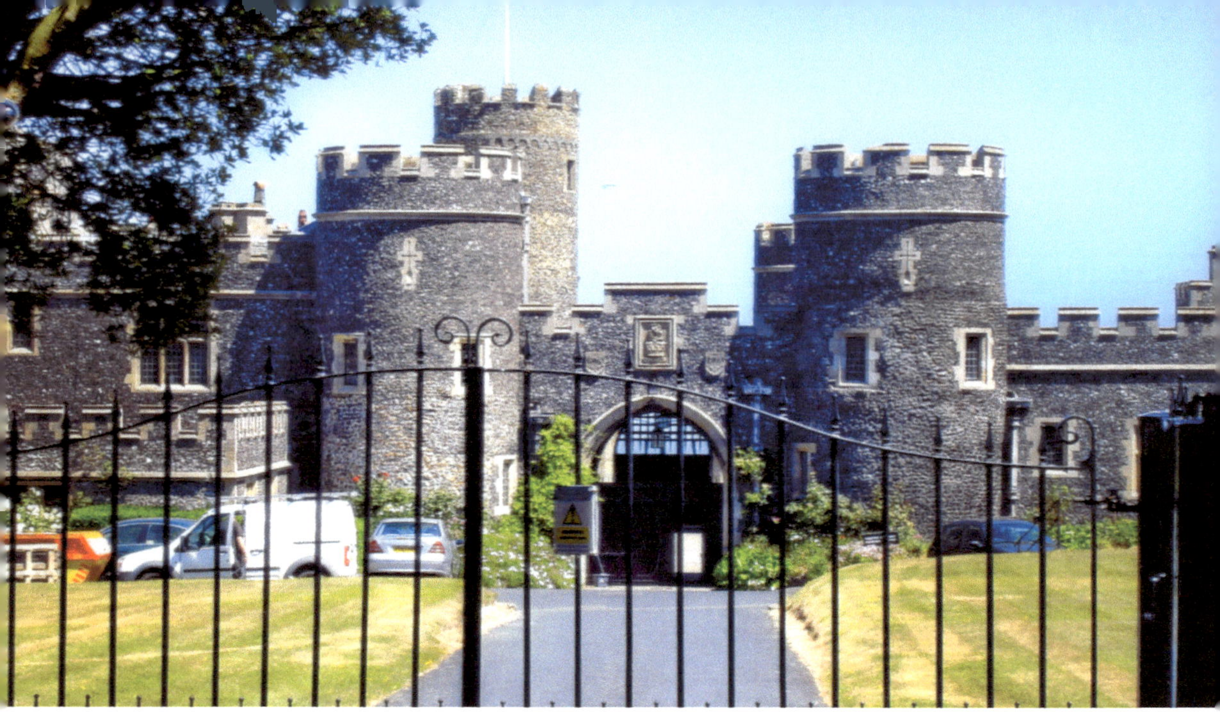

Kingsgate Castle, near Broadstairs.

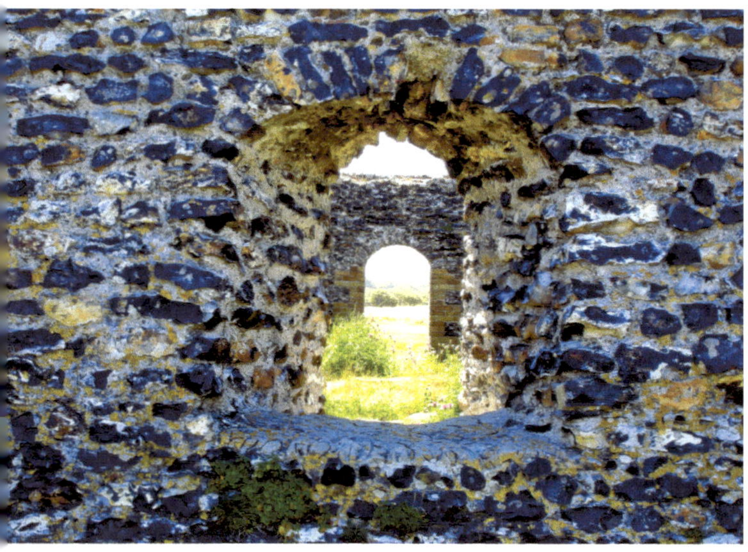

Inside Neptune's Tower at
Kingsgate Bay.

saw the symbol that the key told me indicated simply a 'tower'. So was this an historic monument, an old fort, watchtower or church? The map did not help. You can walk around this ruin, go inside it, give it a thorough looking over, all to no avail. I could see no noticeboard or other information to explain what this structure was. I have since learned, however, that this was another in a series of castellated follies around Kingsgate Bay like the Captain Digby and Kingsgate Castle. Apparently this one once had a central tower and was called Neptune's Tower and had been placed where local legend claimed the fifth-century British King Vortigern once had a fort or watchtower.

North Coast

34. Botany Bay

As the Kent coastline turns to face the Thames Estuary and the North Sea the line of chalk cliffs continues, punctuated by many bays with fine bathing beaches. Perhaps the best of these is the exotically named Botany Bay, which has a Blue Flag beach of soft sand backed by white cliffs notable for their sea caves and chalk stacks.

Botany Bay.

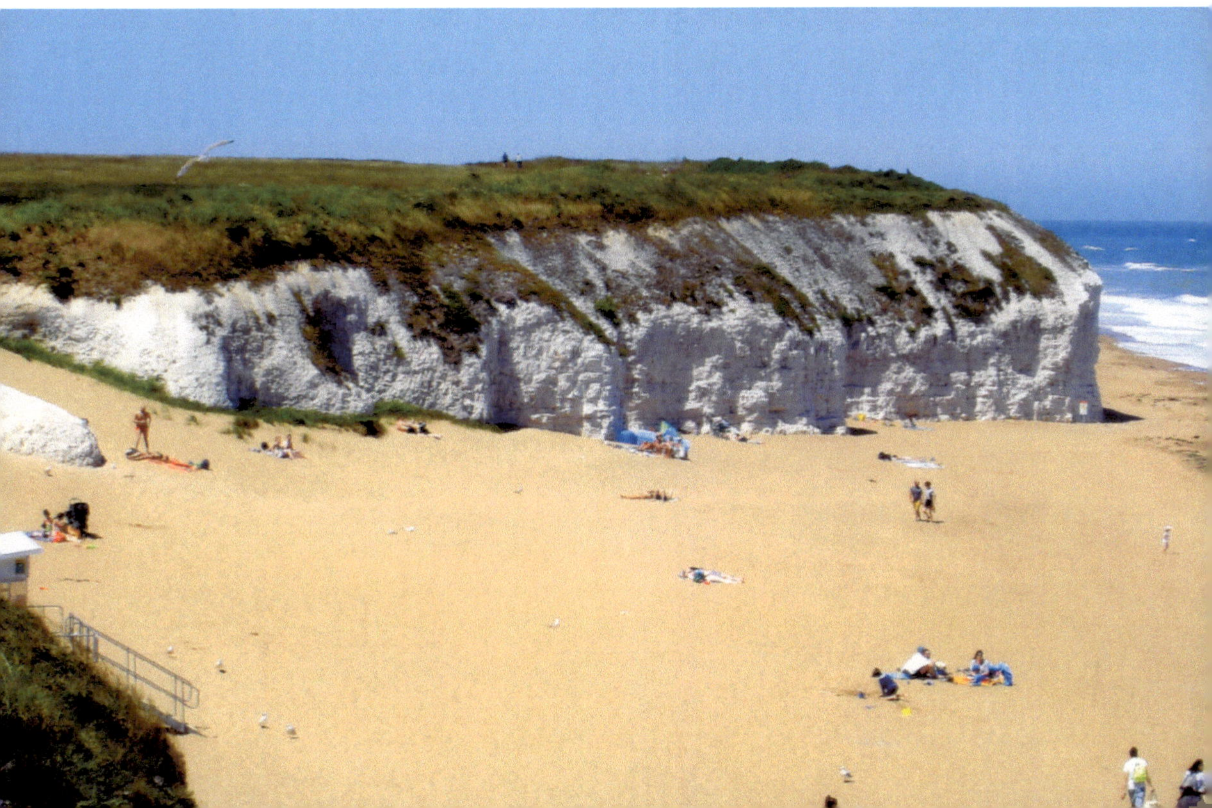

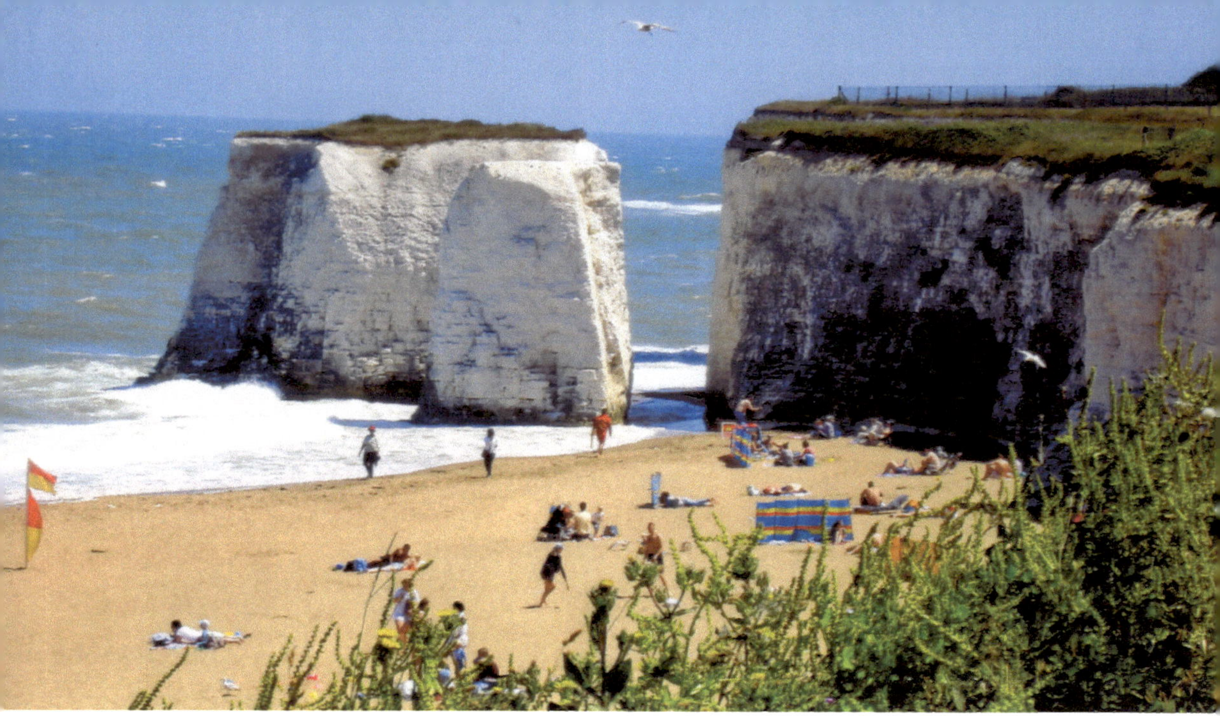

Popular not only with swimmers, sunbathers and families with children, Botany Bay is also popular as a film location and site for commercial photo shoots. I noticed the Botany Bay coastline in the 2010 BBC adaptation of M. R. James's ghost story *Oh Whistle and I'll Come to You* starring John Hurt. Bollywood has even come here, using Botany Bay as a location in the 2012 film *Thaandavam*

The bay has the benefit of being far enough out of town to feel pleasantly remote without being inaccessible. A constant stream of ships passing up and down the Thames Estuary can be seen from here, and in the distance the many whirling windmills of a large offshore wind farm.

A walk or cycle ride of around 2 miles along the Viking Coastal Trail brings you to that seaside Mecca, Margate.

35. Turner Contemporary, Margate

Margate has been the quintessential British seaside resort ever since local resident Benjamin Beale invented the bathing machine back in 1753. Steamboats soon followed, bringing day trippers and holidaymakers down from London every weekend, including sunset-besotted artist J. M. W. Turner who included Margate along with other local places in some of his famous works.

With the coming of the railway the town became renowned as a bucket and spade holiday resort, helped by its golden sandy beaches, seaside fun and from the 1920s onwards its large permanent funfair called Dreamland, particularly notable for its 140-foot-tall big wheel.

By the end of the twentieth century the seaside holiday market had declined markedly, as did the prosperity of Margate along with many other traditional British seaside resorts. However, in common with some of those same resorts, a tide of regeneration – often arts led – brought a welcome change. In Margate this took the form of a revitalisation of the Old Town, helped by the arrival of the fast rail link from St Pancras and the long awaited opening of the stunning Turner Contemporary Gallery on the seafront in 2011.

Here you can view the best of both contemporary and historical art in a rolling programme of exhibitions. There is always at least one work by Turner on display. In addition there are fantastic views across the Bay, including Margate Main Sands, which of course are all sun, sea and sandcastles, along the coast of chalk cliff backed sandy bays toward the distant towers of Reculver and inland the buzzing town of Margate itself. Sitting in the Turner Gallery's outside restaurant seating area on a sunny day, the scene is a vibrant one.

Nearby the Turner Gallery is an information centre at the start of the Harbour Arm, a Georgian stone pier with an 85-foot-tall lighthouse at the end. You can walk along this and enjoy cafés, bobbing fishing boats and more great views. Even Dreamland is back up and running (since 2015), its big wheel now turning again.

Turner Contemporary Gallery, Margate.

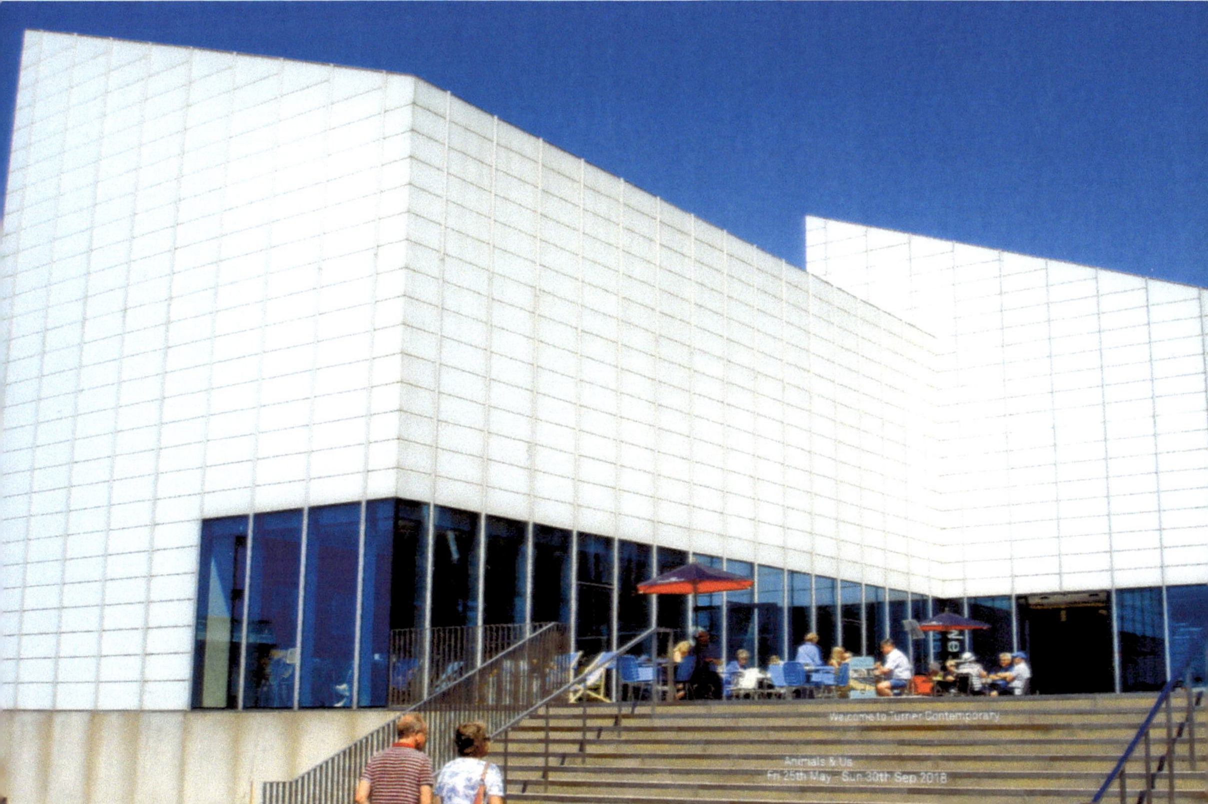

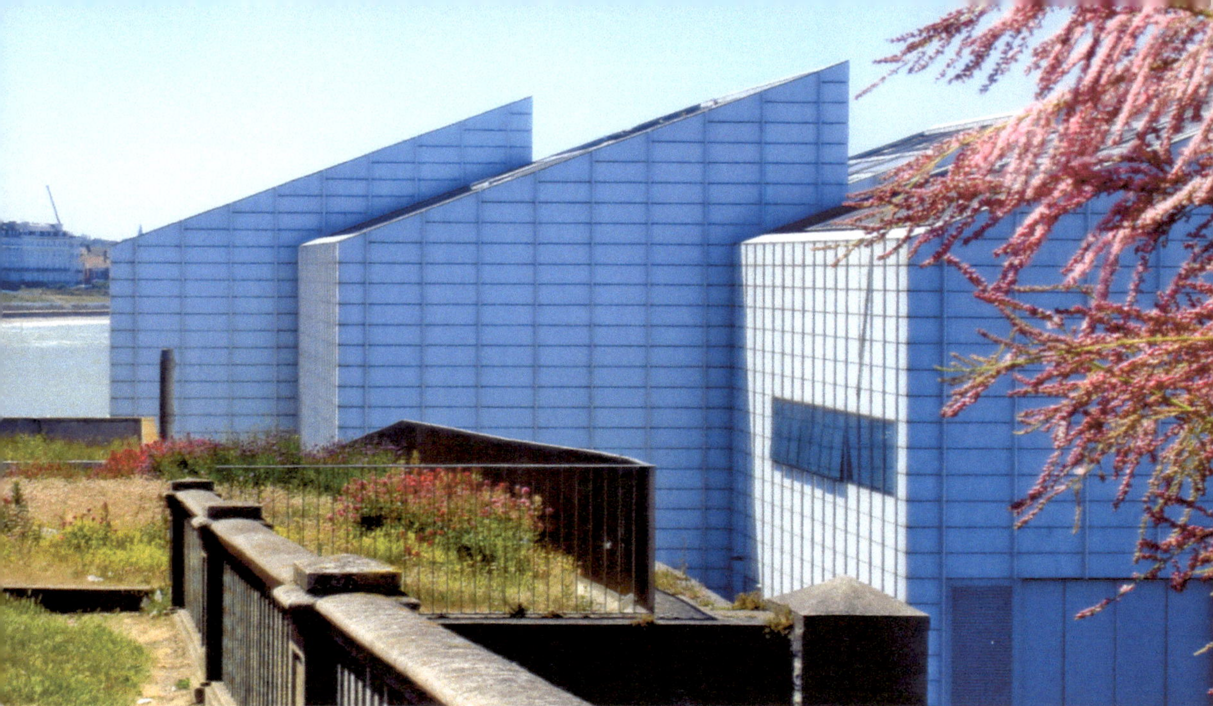

36. Shell Grotto, Margate

This one is something of an enigma. Situated in Margate's Grotto Road, the Shell Grotto is approached by winding steps through chalk walls to an archway where suddenly you see the roof and walls are covered in a myriad of seashells forming impressive patterns. The passageway is some 8 feet high and 70 feet long and ends in a rectangular room around 15 by 20 feet. Above, a dome allows daylight to penetrate down into the grotto illuminating the mosaic of shells, many arranged into star-like patterns. Some of the shells can be identified as coming from nearby beaches, but the majority are flat winkles that are now only found west of Southampton. Who went to the effort of collecting all these shells (estimated to number 4.5 million) to create this grotto and why is a mystery.

The official story is that the grotto was discovered by accident in 1835, its origin unknown. The first definite mention of it seems to be an 1838 newspaper article describing the grotto and announcing its imminent opening as a visitor attraction. There has been speculation that this was some kind of ancient religious site, but it seems more likely to me that it was inspired by other similar creations such as Pope's Grotto in Twickenham (constructed in 1765) or Scott's Grotto in Ware, Hertfordshire, which has been nicknamed 'Fairy Hall'. This latter one was created by John Scott, a Quaker poet, over several years up to

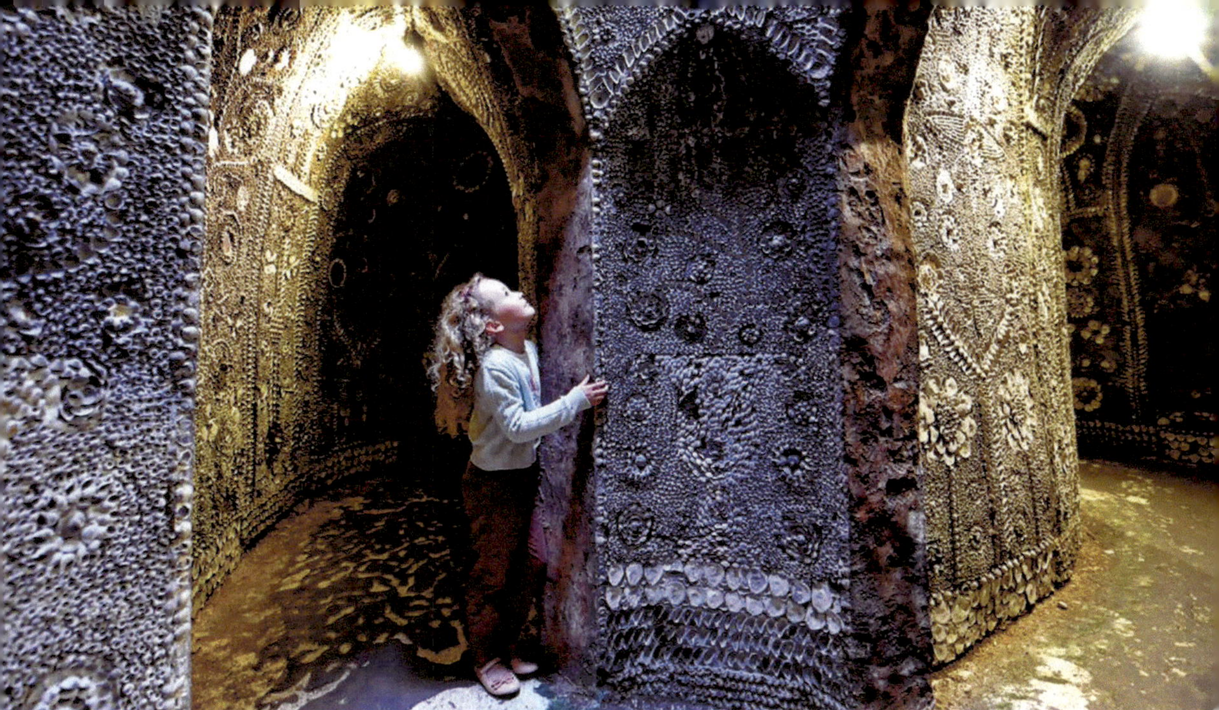

1768 when it was opened and became a popular place to visit. This grotto is the largest in the United Kingdom and has attracted a Grade I listing by English Heritage. Margate's Shell Grotto has also been Grade I listed and has been looked after by the Friends of Shell Grotto since 2008.

Not far away at Northdown Road in Margate are the Margate Caves, which have had various uses over the years but started as chalk/flint mines as is similar with many caves and tunnels in the chalk of southern England. My guess is that the Shell Grotto was created in some pre-existing chalk mine workings either as a rich man's folly during the eighteenth century (possibly the 1760s) or deliberately as a tourist attraction in the 1830s. Either way, similar grottos may well have served as its inspiration (or vice versa).

Undeniably, the Shell Grotto is an intriguing place and well worth a visit. It may not be as ancient as some claim but no less wonderful for that and definitely one of the 'gems' of East Kent.

37. Reculver Towers

There can be few sights on the Kent coast as starkly impressive as the twin towers of St Mary's Church at Reculver. The two large Norman towers are on a relatively flat coastline and visible from many miles away, always seemingly much nearer to you than they actually are.

Seen from the outside seating area of the Turner Contemporary in Margate or out of the window of a pub on Herne Bay seafront, the distant structures exert an allure that if acted upon will lead to a walk or cycle that will prove much longer than you ever expected.

When you finally get there, Reculver Towers are no less impressive and you will learn more about them. Originally there was a Roman fort on this site, built around the late second to mid-third century AD to guard the northern end of the Wantsum Chancel, which at the time separated mainland Kent from the Isle of Thanet. Later, in 669, a church was built within the walls of the Roman fort using material from the by then disused building. A monastery was also established, but Viking raids during the ninth century led to its abandonment. The impressive church towers are of twelfth-century origin, with the connecting chancel frame built in the thirteenth century. Today the towers form one of the country's more spectacular medieval ruins, bettered in my opinion only by

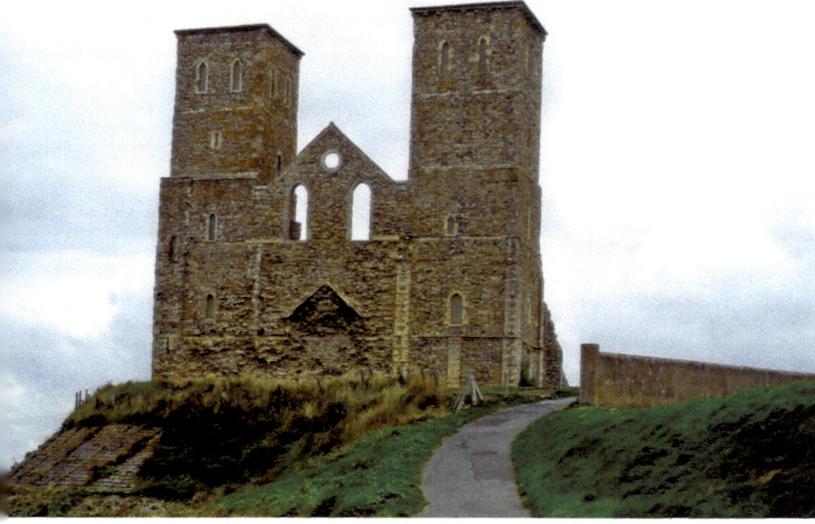

Reculver Towers, looking east.

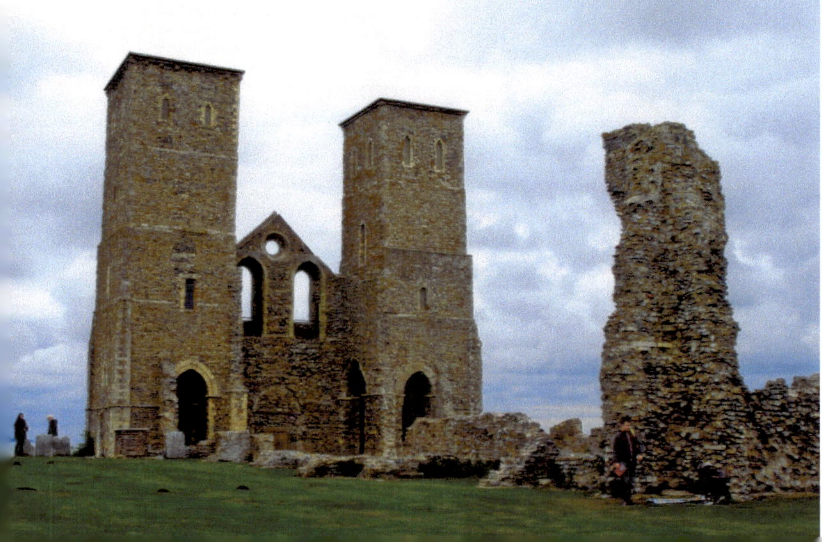

Reculver Towers, looking west.

Whitby Abbey on the Yorkshire coast. Most of the body of the church has fallen victim to coastal erosion over the last 300 years along with much of the village of Reculver, which now lies beneath the sea hundreds of yards off the current coastline. I remember first learning of the lost church and village as a child and feeling a strange sense of melancholy at the sight of the flat, grey sea concealing the remains of a village. I think I was told about the devastating floods of 1953 that afflicted this coast at the same time and the idea of familiar places being engulfed by the sea filled me with dread for years afterwards, especially when I lived below sea level on Romney Marsh for a couple of years.

Reculver Towers are now protected from the sea by sturdy sea defences that are maintained by Trinity House as the towers are an important navigational aid. If walking or cycling the towers can be reached by following the Thanet Coastal Path, which runs from Ramsgate to Herne Bay.

38. Herne Bay

I first remember Herne Bay from childhood day trips with the family. I paddled with my cousins on the beach, in sea that seemed to remain very shallow for a long way out. This shallow paddling water on warm sand was a great pleasure and made Herne Bay Beach ideal for young children. This was back in the heyday of the British seaside holiday. Like many such resorts, Herne Bay faded somewhat over the years, and in 1978 even its pier – the second longest in Britain after Southend – was largely destroyed in a winter storm. The beach and seafront were covered for days with the smashed and washed up remains of the wooden pier, whose pier head still stands forlornly stranded out to sea.

Come the twenty-first century and Herne Bay has looked up rather well. The town remains a family seaside resort, but at the quieter end of the spectrum these days. There are amusements, a mini funfair on the remaining pier stub and a fine clock tower on the seafront – 80 feet tall and built in 1837. Colourful beach huts follow the shoreline and a harbour enclosed by a wall called Neptune's Arm allows small boats to moor. Looking out beyond the Arm and indeed all the way to Reculver or Whitstable, the thirty or so turbines of the Kentish Flats offshore wind farm dominate the horizon. Personally, I'm in favour of this clean, if intermittent, source of energy and don't find the turbines unattractive.

One of the things I like about Herne Bay is its sense of healthy, breezy spaciousness both along the seafront where the Victorian houses are set back from the sea wall and in the pedestrianised Mortimer Street that runs parallel with the seafront.

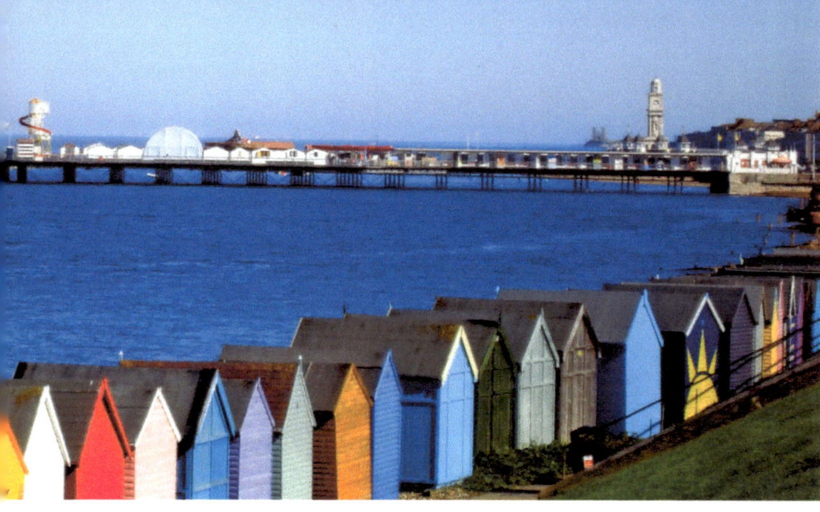

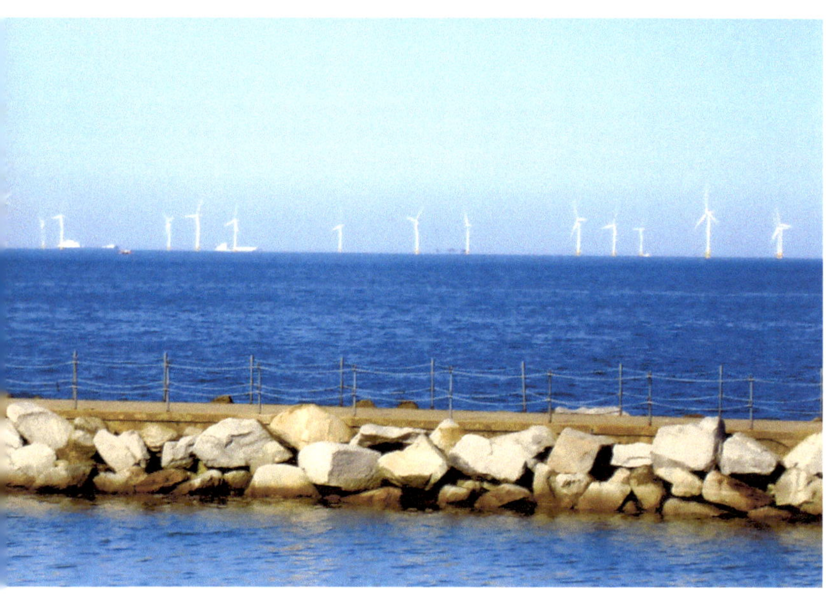

There is a good walk east to Bishopstone Glen, a tree- and fern-filled cleft in the cliffs with steps to the sea, and to Reculver beyond. To the west lies the busy, working seaside town of Whitstable, our next port of call.

39. Whitstable

Follow the beach huts westwards out of Herne Bay and after a couple of miles there are more beach huts as you approach Whitstable. Green slopes and beach huts seem to dominate this stretch of coast as far as Tankerton. The large

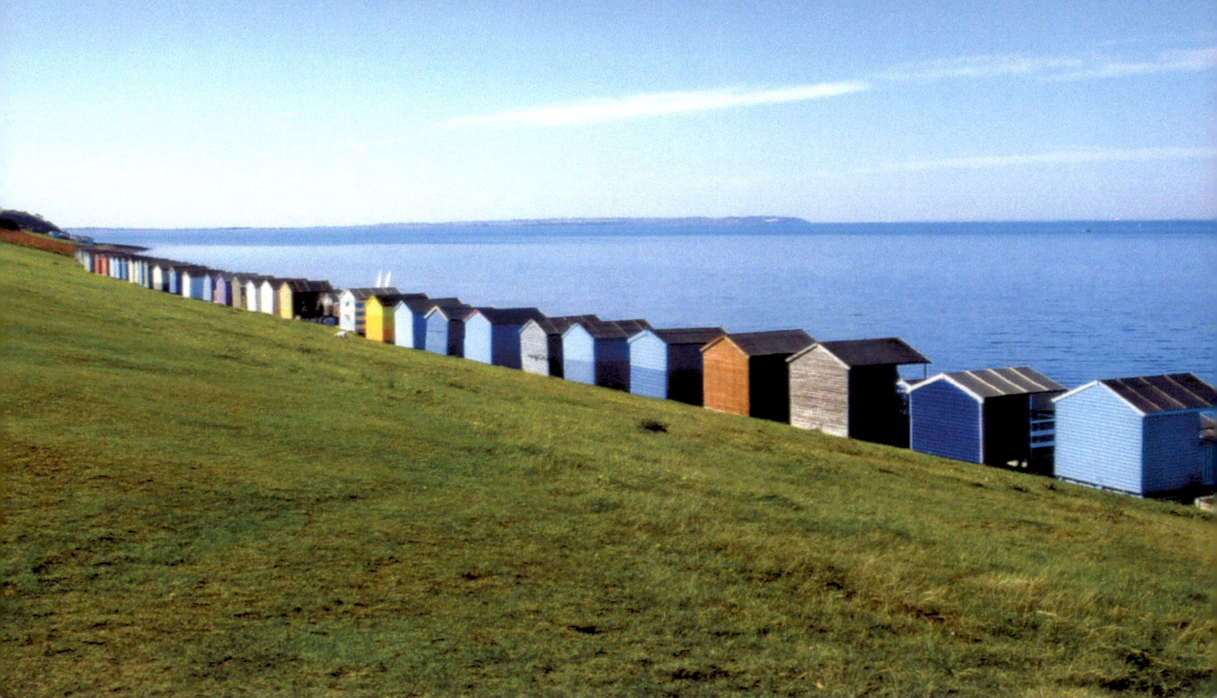

castellated building on the clifftop here overlooking Whitstable, known as Whitstable Castle, is actually a mansion house built in around 1790 rather than a military structure. The surrounding gardens are a popular place to have tea sitting in the sun.

Descending into Whitstable itself is an interesting prospect. This is not really a resort; its beaches are shingle and divided by wooden groynes, weatherboarded cottages pressed hard against the seafront and there are no great conglomerations of amusements, no funfair and no pier. This is a working seaside town, mostly centred around the oyster-harvesting industry. Oysters have been harvested here since Roman times and today there is a popular annual Oyster Festival. The oyster hatchery here is the largest in Europe and has recently been expanding along the coast at Seasalter. The popularity of this seafood was boosted from the 1830s onward with the coming of the railway. George Stephenson's *Invicta*, a twin to his famous *Rocket*, hauled the first passenger-carrying railway service in the country between Canterbury and Whitstable. The railway has long since closed and been converted into the Crab and Winkle Way cycle path.

Whitstable Harbour is a buzzing hub of activity. Cargo ships dock (timber and aggregates are the main commercial business), fishing boats unload, and pleasure trips into the Thames Estuary set off to see the Kentish Flats Windfarm turbines at close quarters or the Maunsell Forts.

The Maunsell Forts are rusty old Second World War gun emplacements on stilts. In the 1960s they were used by a pirate radio station; today they stand abandoned, though much visited. From the shore the forts look like a line of full stops on the horizon. Close up they present an eerie spectacle, resembling H. G. Well's Martian war machines from his 1898 novel *The War of the Worlds*.

One of the most pleasant ways to venture out and explore the Thames Estuary is by taking a trip on the 120-year-old Thames sailing barge *Greta*, which goes out from Whitstable Harbour.

If you don't fancy a boat trip, there are oysters and seafood galore at numerous outlets around the harbour. It's always buzzing, even on an otherwise quiet autumn afternoon, as I found out.

Away from the harbour Whitstable is interesting in other ways. Narrow alleys connect the town to the seafront – some with amusing names such as Squeeze Gut Alley. There are eateries and pubs such as The Old Neptune, which is actually situated on the shingle beach. Whitstable has become a bit of a magnet for those on a day trip wanting to browse in antique or second-hand bookshops, looking for a good pub lunch and perhaps visiting an art gallery.

For me, waiting for the bus back to Canterbury, the former cinema (now a Wetherspoons pub) named after a famous Whitstable resident and star of many a Hammer horror film, Peter Cushing, provides a suitable watering hole.

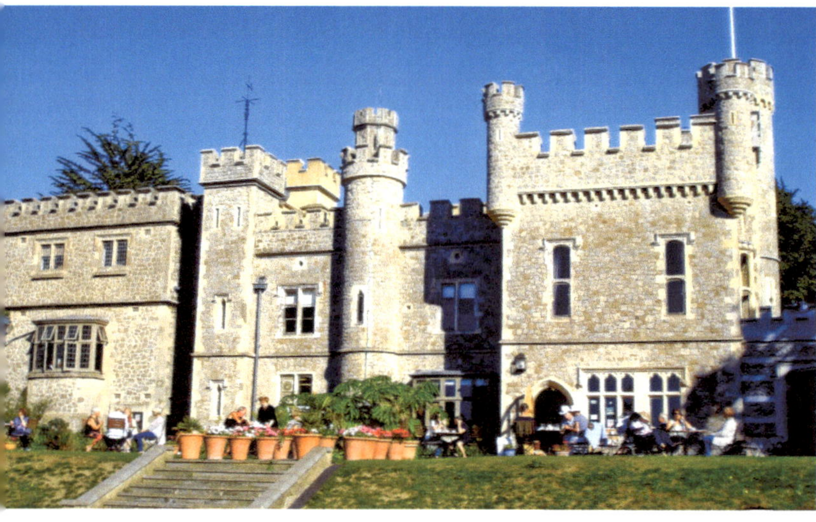

Whitstable Castle.

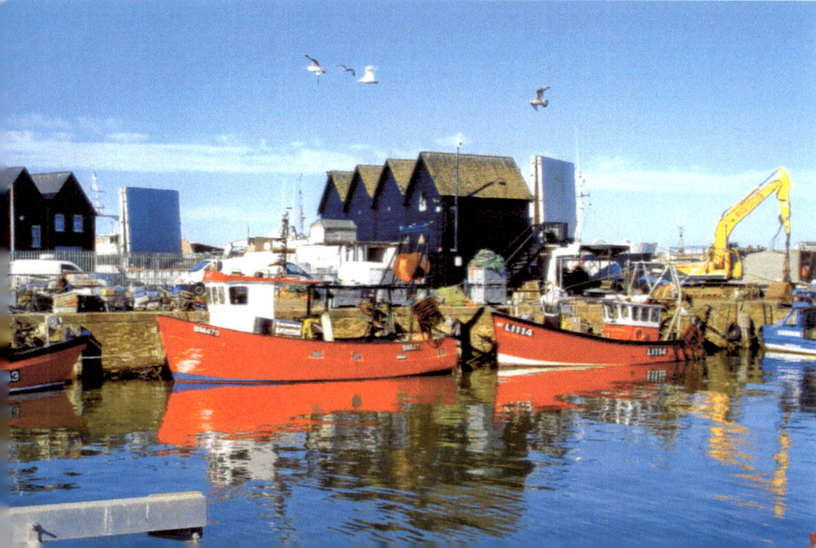

Whitstable Harbour.

Canterbury and Countryside

40. Canterbury

Undoubtedly the 'capital' of East Kent – for history, visible heritage, shopping, visitor attractions, arts, education and sheer bustling vibrancy.

Most, though not all of what Canterbury offers, lies within the ancient walls. These are originally Roman, though most of what we see today is thirteenth to fourteenth century. These walls had four gates, one of which is still visible with its sturdy medieval towers at Westgate.

The city inside the walls is a vibrant mix of quality shopping, hordes of visitors rubbing shoulders with numerous students from four universities and other quality educational establishments (such as the famous King's School founded 1,400 years ago), and history and heritage galore provided by a range of museums and other sights.

There is the Roman museum that recreates what life was like in the city around AD 300 with full-scale representations of Roman shops and a Roman mosaic pavement as its centrepiece.

The Canterbury Museum includes a whole section on Rupert Bear as part of its overview of the city's history. The Canterbury Tales recreates the sights, sounds and smells of the medieval Canterbury of Geoffrey Chaucer, and the Beaney House of Art and Knowledge includes a gallery devoted to local rural scenes artist Sidney Cooper. The Marlow Theatre is a popular venue near the river with the Greyfriars Chapel and Franciscan Gardens opposite, fronted by a large metal theatrical mask by sculptor Rick Kirby. Walking and boat tours depart from the King's Bridge past the half-timbered 'Weavers' houses and along the tranquil Stour. King's Bridge also has the Eastbridge pilgrims hospital/hostel. Originally catering for medieval pilgrims heading to the shrine of St Thomas Becket, it is now partially open to the public and still provides accommodation in the form of self-contained flats for local elderly people. Dominating it all, however, is the world famous mother church of Anglicanism, Canterbury Cathedral.

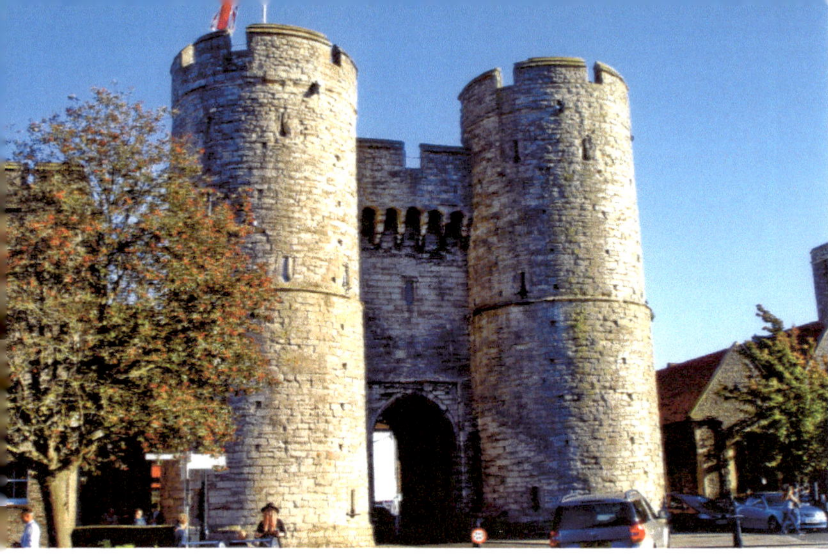

Westgate Towers, Canterbury.

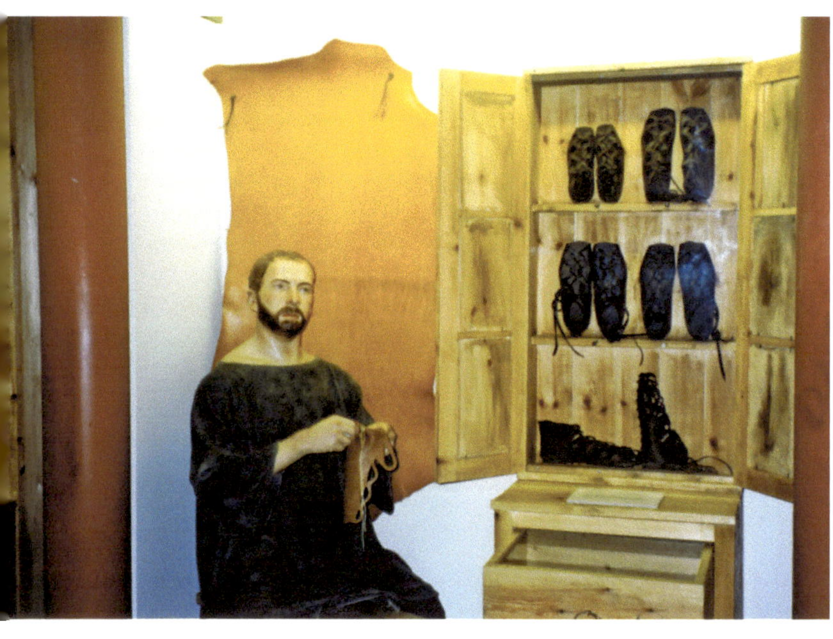

Shoe shop in Roman Museum.

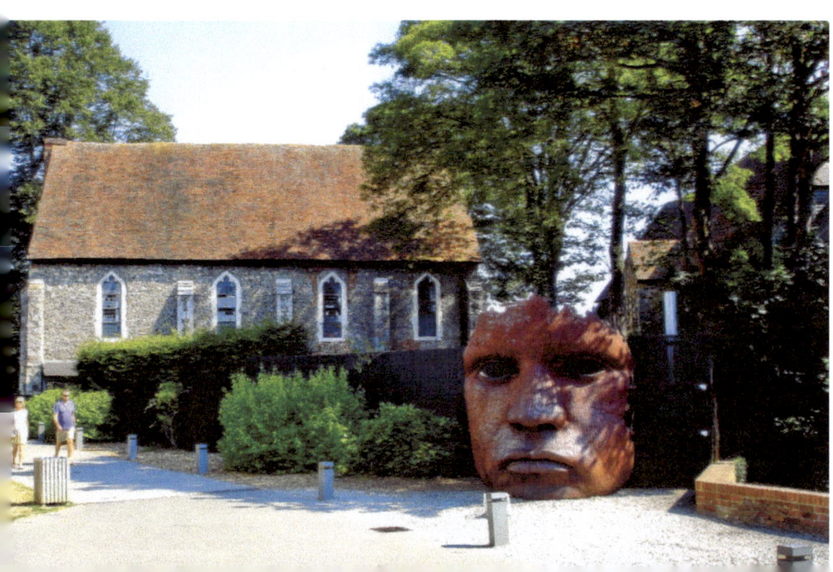

Greyfriars Chapel with theatrical mask sculpture.

41. Canterbury Cathedral

Founded in AD 597 by St Augustine, the first Canterbury Cathedral was completed in 602 and the process then continued throughout the Middle Ages. Most of what you see today dates from the twelfth century onwards, particularly since 1170 following the murder in the cathedral of Archbishop Thomas Becket. Not long after his death miracles began to be attributed to him and pilgrims came from far and wide to visit his shrine. Such pilgrimages were, of course, the inspiration for Geoffrey Chaucer's *The Canterbury Tales*. It is said that Canterbury Cathedral has been the most visited building in Britain for the last 850 years. It is easy to imagine the awe this immense and beautiful structure evoked in the medieval pilgrim when glimpsing it from afar or from the narrow shopping streets of Canterbury.

The tall central tower known as the Bell Harry Tower is 234 feet in height and was built in 1495, a sight as sacred to many as a national icon as the White Cliffs of Dover or Big Ben. Inside the immense building are the tombs of numerous kings, saints and archbishops including Edward I, the Black Prince, Henry IV and Thomas Becket, whose shrine is here too. Of more specialist interest, perhaps, are the collection of 'green men' and other interesting sculptures, for which this is a prime site of importance. There are numerous examples adorning the curved ceiling of the cloisters, which are accessible from the main building. Art exhibitions are hosted here too. On my latest visit a huge glass chandelier called the 'Boat of Remembrance' hung in the cathedral's nave. This was composed of 100 clear glass amphorae suspended in the shape of a ship, each one representing a year of remembrance since the Armistice of 1918. This was one of a series of installations by Philip Baldwin and Monica Guggisberg and exhibited together with the title *Under an Equal Sky*.

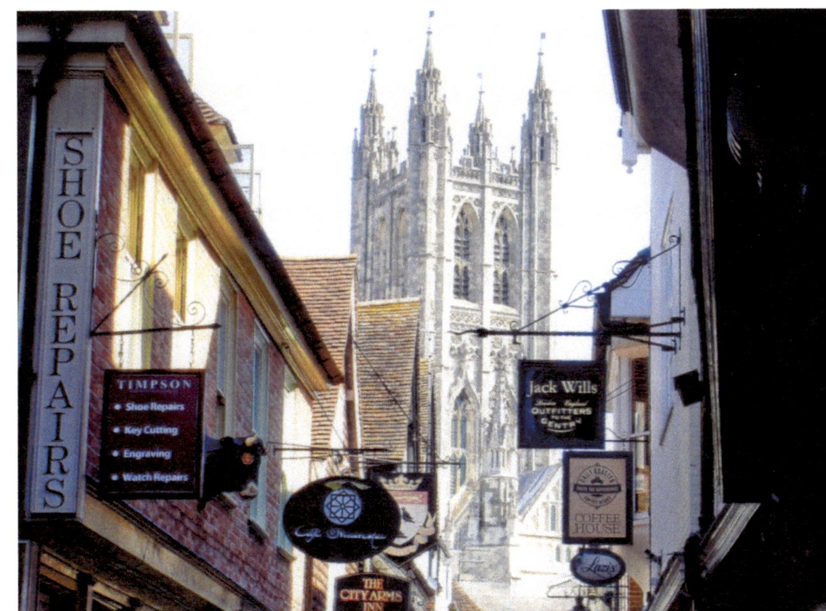

Canterbury Cathedral towers over the city's narrow streets.

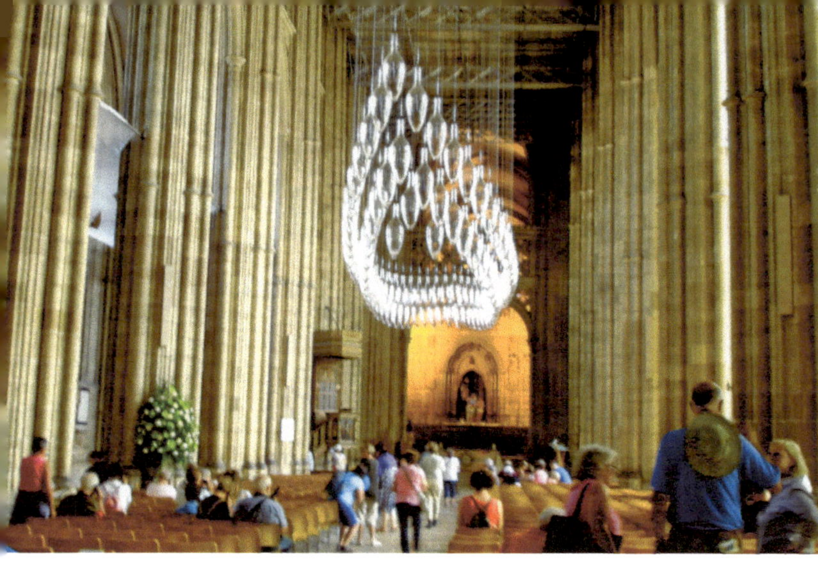

The cathedral continues to evolve. Today eighteen stonemasons conserve the work of their medieval colleagues and create new carvings as intricate and beautiful as the originals. The stone used is limestone, originally Caen stone but increasingly from other sources such as Bath and Ancaster.

Canterbury Cathedral is more than just a building, it is a site of international importance. Ecclesiastically speaking, of course, because it is the seat of the Archbishop of Canterbury, but also because of its heritage value. It forms part of a UNESCO World Heritage Site that extends beyond the city walls to include St Augustine's Abbey and St Martin's Church, to where we will now go.

42. St Martin's Church, Canterbury

Heading south from Canterbury Cathedral, beyond the city walls, a small garden contains two statues – those of Queen Bertha and King Ethelbert. It was they who were instrumental in St Augustine coming to Kent to bring Christianity to its inhabitants and eventually on to the rest of Britain.

Queen Bertha started the ball rolling upon her marriage to Ethelbert. She was of Frankish descent and Christian persuasion, and as part of the marriage settlement required a place to follow her faith. A small church that had been used by Christians in Roman times was made available to her. This was just outside the walls of the city and became what we know as St Martin's, the oldest parish church in the English-speaking world.

Just as Canterbury Cathedral is the mother church of worldwide Anglicanism, so St Martin's is recognised in turn as the mother church of the cathedral. It is the earliest of the three buildings that are included in the UNESCO Canterbury World Heritage Site. The chancel and some Roman bricks date back to around

AD 350. Later came St Augustine's Abbey just down the hill, founded by Augustine shortly after his arrival, along with the cathedral. Queen Bertha, King Ethelbert and a host of other notables are buried at St Augustine's Abbey, which today is a ruin but is open to the public and has a very good visitor centre.

St Martin's Church is not a ruin and is very much in use today, having been in continuous use for most of the last 1,700 years. It has an interesting graveyard and a little booklet of who is buried where can be found in the church. Apparently the most sought after grave is that of Mary Tourtel, the author of the popular Rupert Bear children's comic strip stories.

St Martin's can be found in North Holmes Road, just off St Martin's Hill on the road towards Sandwich. A little further up the hill, in Littlebourne Road,

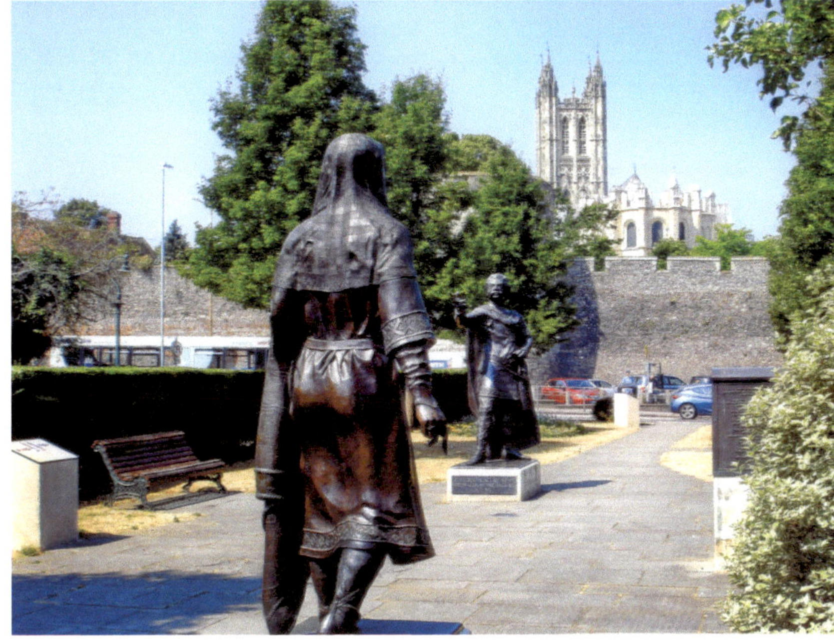

Statues of Queen Bertha and King Ethelbert with cathedral in background.

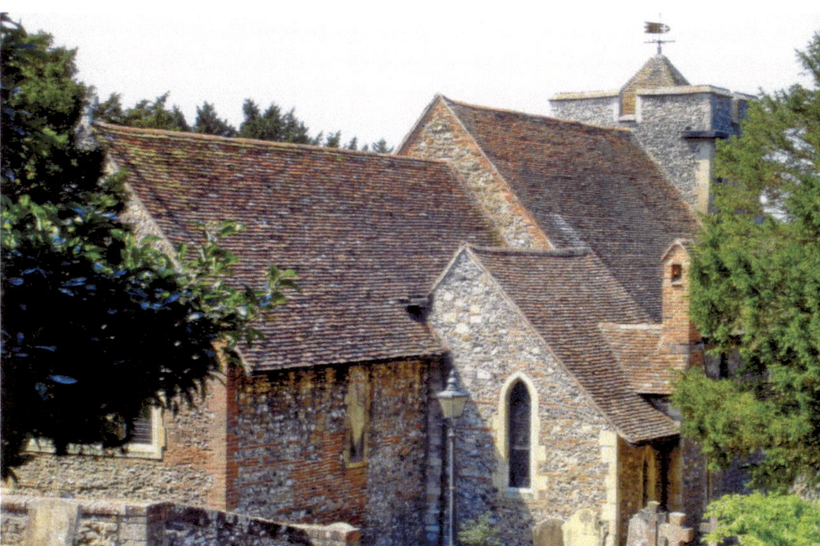

St Martin's Church.

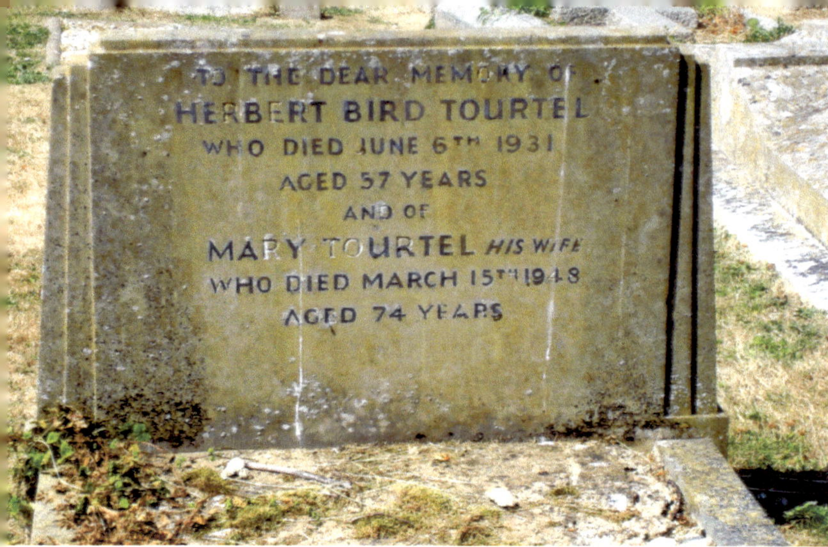

Grave of Mary Tourtel and husband.

my mother once lived as a child. She married my father at St Martin's, which was of course her local parish church, so the place is obviously of personal significance to me.

43. Wingham

Continuing on the Canterbury to Sandwich road for a few miles brings us eventually to the village of Wingham, visible from afar by virtue of its tall conical church steeple. The tree-lined main road leads through a pleasant village with a number of very old half-timbered houses, including one built in 1286.

Wingham has more than once earned the Kentish 'Best Kept Village' accolade and it is easy to see why, despite the almost constant flow of traffic these days. The lovely wrought-iron village sign sums up its attractions: the earlier mentioned medieval buildings, surrounding woodland walks, St Mary's Church with its landmark steeple, and dinosaurs.

The mention of dinosaurs is a reference to the Wingham Wildlife Park a short distance outside the village in the Sandwich direction. This popular visitor attraction contains a wide selection of animals and birds and opportunities to get up close to or interact with some of the creatures here, but dinosaurs? Surprisingly, yes, there are a few life-sized animatronic dinosaurs moving about (to a limited extent anyway), much to the delight of children, who for at least the last couple of generations seem perpetually fascinated by these prehistoric creatures.

I have long been acquainted with Wingham; my mother was born here and often recounted happy childhood memories of her time in the village.

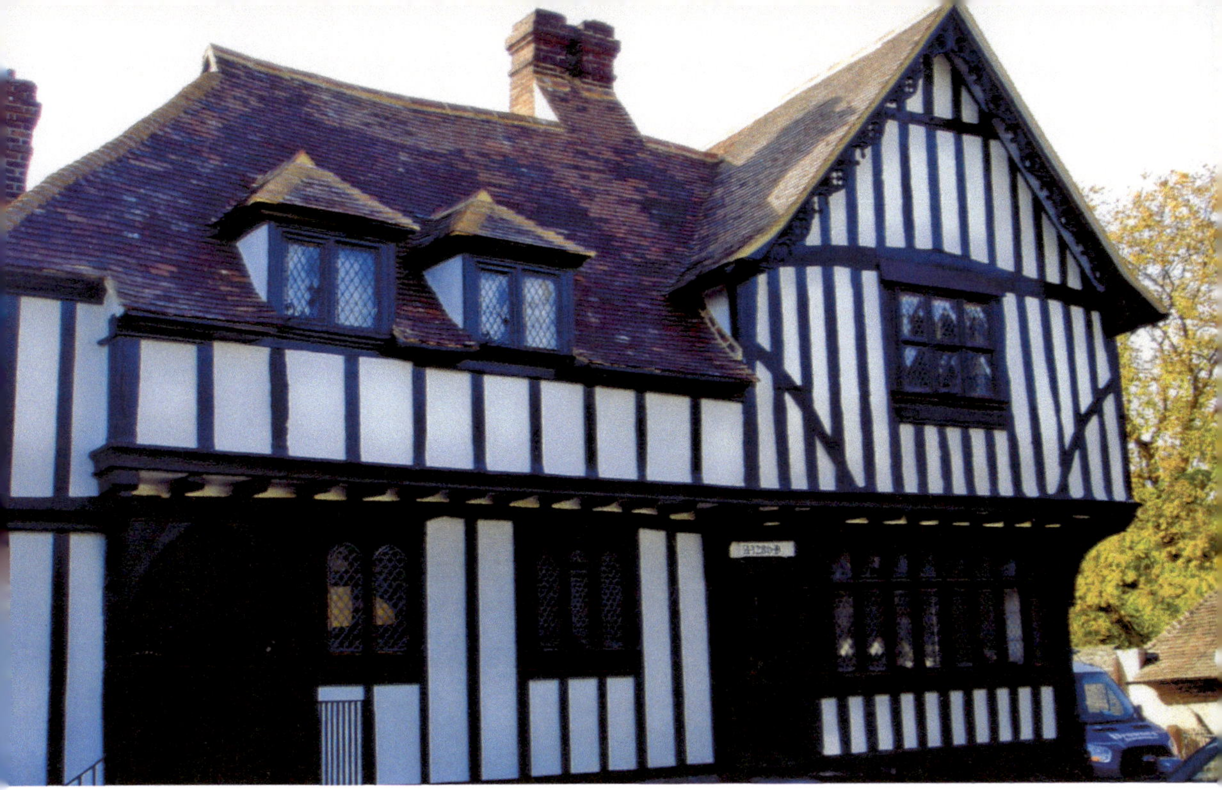

Above: House built in 1286, Wingham.

Below: Wingham village sign.

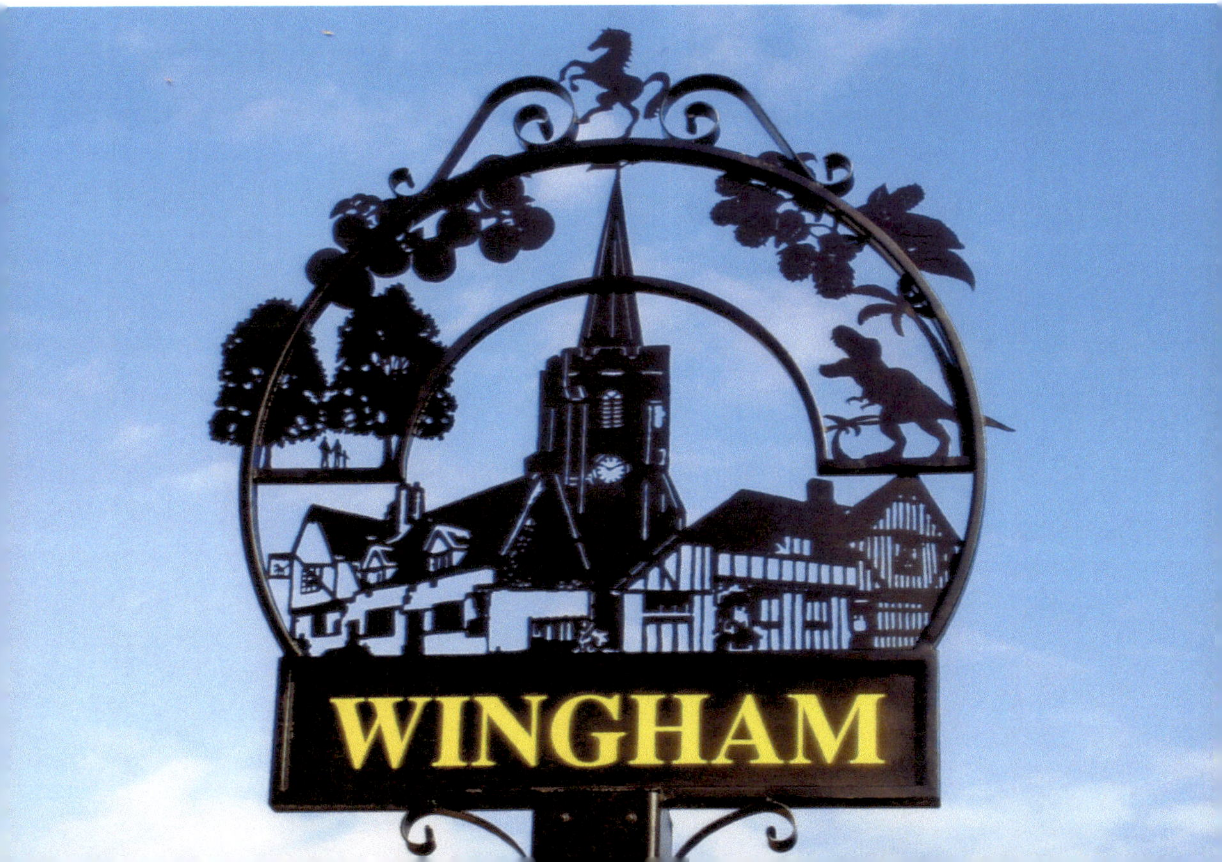

44. Patrixbourne

Located 3 miles south-east of Canterbury and away from the busy main roads, a small but picturesque village straddles the Little Stour, a tributary of the Stour that runs through Canterbury. It has been described as the prettiest village in Kent by a Canadian friend who tries to visit it whenever he is over here.

A straddle of half-timbered houses and cottages follow the quiet minor road, one of which crosses the Little Stour by ford, a pleasing feature that caters for walkers by a small footbridge. The cottages and larger houses give the impression of being of Tudor vintage; in fact, the timberwork was added in the mid-nineteenth century, but of course it is still visually pleasing.

A tall conical steeple sits atop the Norman church of St Mary, which stands in a tranquil spot next to the river, which can be seen from the graveyard. The church is constructed of Caen stone and is noted for the fine stone carvings that frame the main doorway.

Eastwards from Patrixbourne a pleasant walk goes to Bekesbourne and on to Littlebourne, following the course of the river. The path passes through old parkland and pleasant orchards to the ruined Well Chapel. Once part of a now vanished manor house, this medieval building stands near a hidden spring next to dense woodland and fields of grazing cattle. The ivy and brambles attempting to cover it just add to its allure, like somewhere from a fairy tale.

Little Stour ford, Patrixbourne.

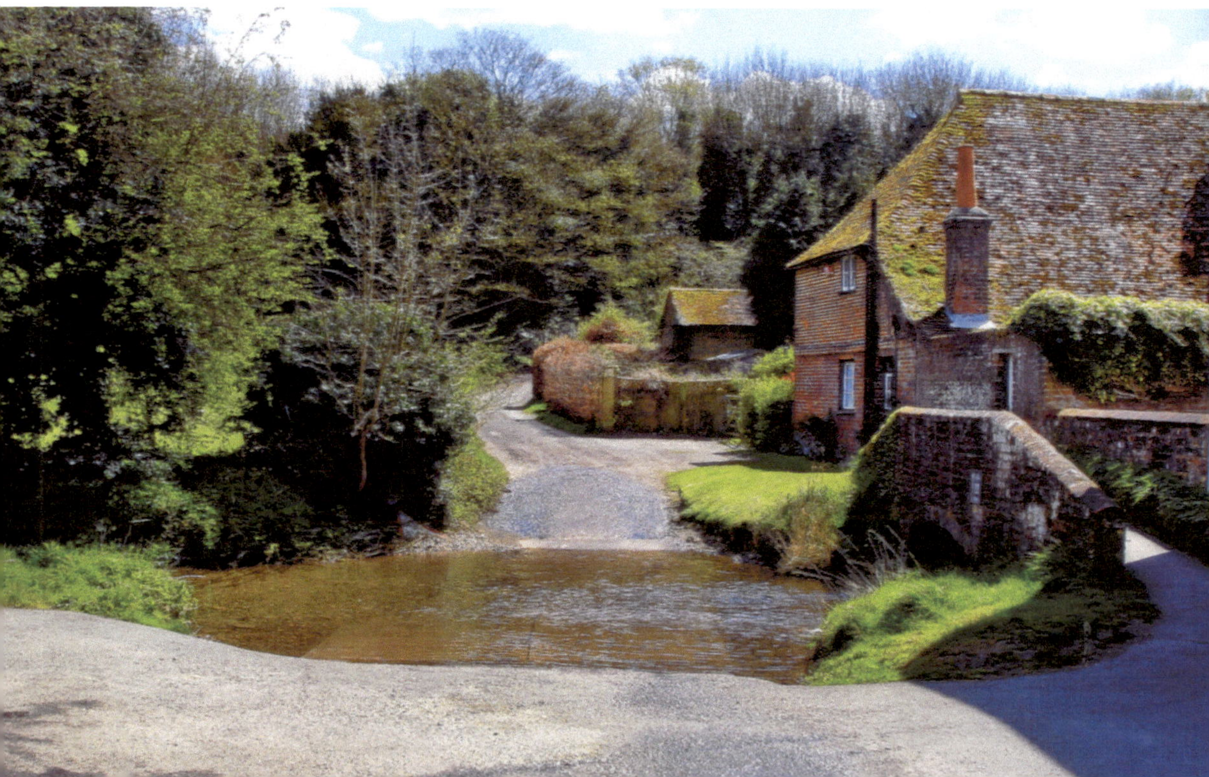

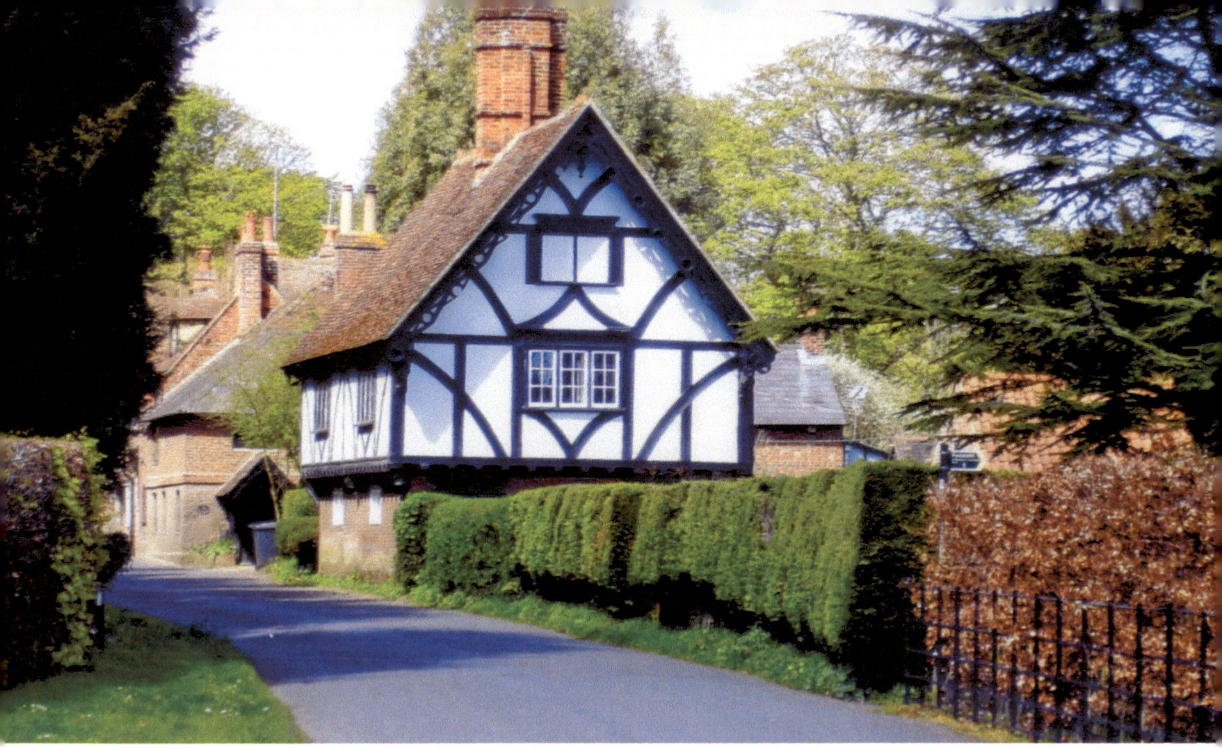

Cottages, Patrixbourne.

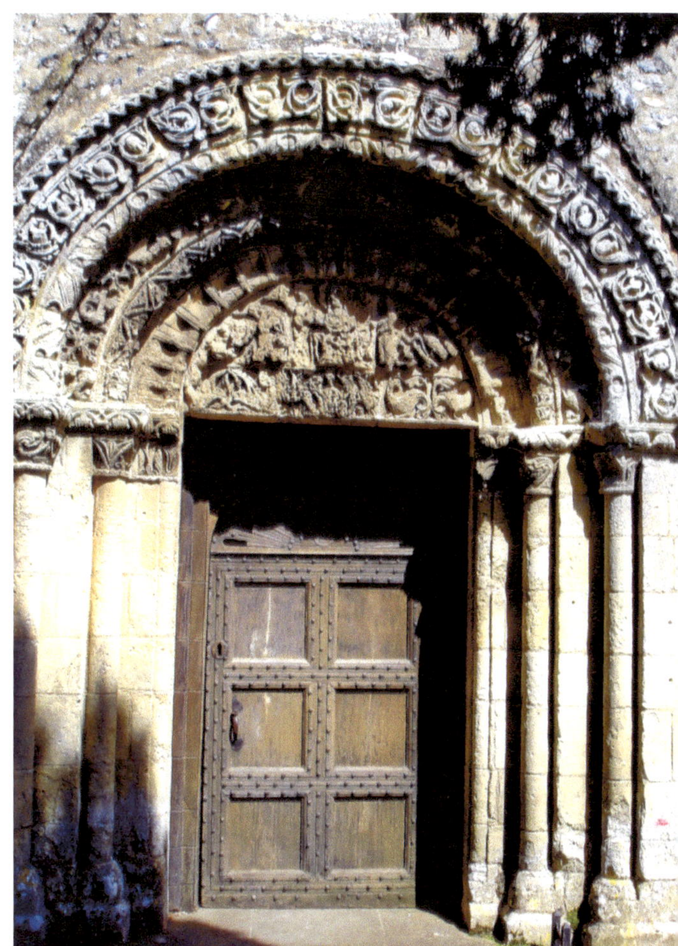

Norman church doorway and
carvings, Patrixbourne.

45. Denton – Ingoldsby Country

The picturesque village of Denton lies 10 miles south of Canterbury on the Folkestone road. The half-timbered houses around the tiny village green, the smell of wood smoke drifting from the nearby public house, the partially glimpsed grandeur of Denton Court and the nearby church of St Mary Magdalene through mushroom-carpeted woodland combine to create a powerful, brooding atmosphere beneath the surrounding hills.

Such spirit of place often inspires tales of mystery and imagination, such has certainly been the case with Denton and its surrounding countryside. The area between here and the main Canterbury to Dover road in the past has been referred to as 'witch haunted' or 'magic ridden'. Place names such as Ghost Hill and Puckland Woods nearer to Dover mystify and intrigue, and local pubs claim to be haunted.

No wonder avid collector of local folklore Richard Harris Barham found plenty of material for his erudite and humorous collection of prose and poetry known as *The Ingoldbsy Legends* (published in 1840 under the pseudonym Thomas Ingoldsby). Barham was born in Burgate, Canterbury, in 1788 and soon inherited the attractive Jacobean farmhouse known as Tappington Hall in Denton in 1796. The current house was built in 1628 and soon boasted a ghost of its own, the result of a clash between two brothers on the staircase in which one was killed. A sword cut is still visible today in the bannister of the staircase, allegedly from this encounter. Barham himself set a ghost story in the house entitled *The Spectre of Tappington* in which former owner 'Bad Sir Giles' was found one morning 'a blackened and swollen corpse'. Ever afterwards he was said to haunt the hall, stealing the breeches of house guests.

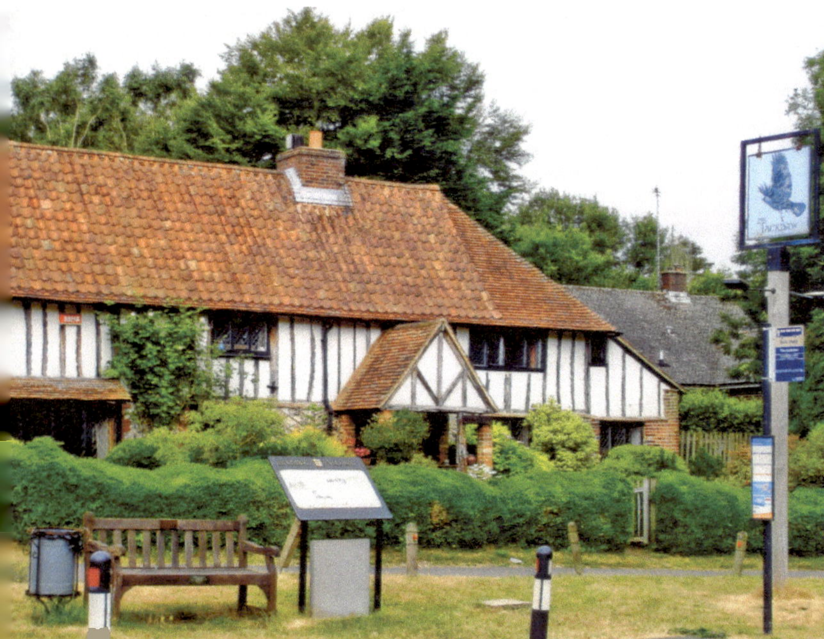

Denton village centre.

Other tales in *The Ingoldsby Legends* were set locally, including *Mrs Botherby's Story – The Leech of Folkestone* in which he describes witches screaming as they flew above Dymchurch Wall on their broomsticks; *The Hand of Glory*, a macabre tale set on Barham Down; and *The Jackdaw of Rheims*, a tale of a bird that stole a cardinal's ring, which is remembered in Denton's pub name. This pub, The Jackdaw, incidentally, featured in the 1969 film *The Battle of Britain*, which was largely filmed locally with an all-star cast and accompanied by a memorable Ron Goodwin film theme.

My favourite 'Ingoldsby Legend' is *The Witches Frolic*, the misadventure of a young boozer/womaniser, Rob Gilpin, who encounters a group of partying witches at the old Knights Hospitaller Preceptory at nearby Swingfield. Very well written and jolly good fun, it would make a good short film I think.

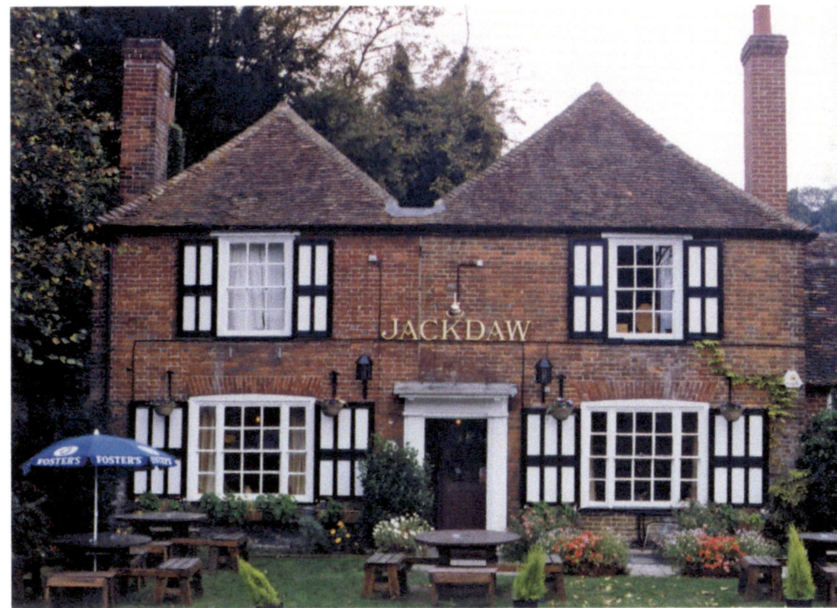

The Jackdaw public house, Denton.

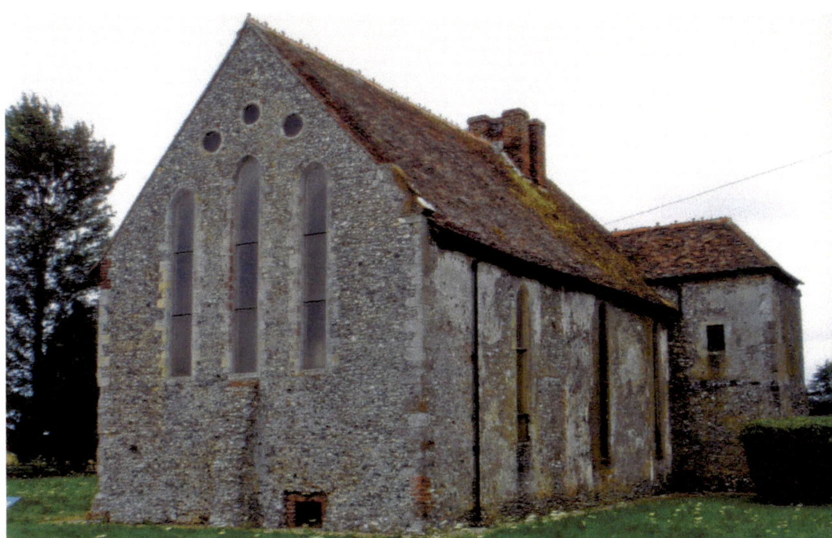

St John's Preceptory, Swingfield, which features in *The Witches Frolic.*

46. Paddlesworth

A few miles south, signposted from Hawkinge, the little hamlet of Paddlesworth can be found. At an altitude of around 650 feet, this is apparently Kent's highest village (though not its highest point, that honour belongs to an 824-foot-high hill near Biggin Hill) and contains its highest church. The parish covers just 1 square mile with a population of between thirty and forty people, just a few houses, a farm, a church and a pub. Hence perhaps the little ditty that hangs in the pub: 'Highest Church, Lowest Steeple, Poorest Parish, Fewest People'.

The pub, called The Cat and Custard Pot, was a favourite with pilots from the nearby RAF airfield at Hawkinge during the Second World War. As such there is an abundance of Battle of Britain memorabilia, including a large model Spitfire hanging from the ceiling. Just down the hill is the Kent Battle of Britain Museum if you want a lot more of this sort of thing. In the pub, next to the ditty mentioned above, hangs (or it did when I was last there) a large heavy key. This can be borrowed to go and open up the nearby St Oswald's Church (the only church in Kent devoted to this Northumbrian king and Christian martyr). The name may indicate that its founding dates back to the time of St Ethelburga, the former Queen of Northumbria who became abbess of nearby Lyminge Monastery from AD 635 to 647. She had been previously the queen of Oswald's predecessor, Edwin.

Inside, St Oswald's presents a cosy, quite basic church interior built in Norman times, mostly of flint. It is, I can confidently say, one of the most beautiful and tranquil small churches I have ever entered. The atmosphere is both calm and powerful and highly recommended to those who like to visit our sacred spaces. A booklet for just 20p explains the history and architecture of this wonderful little place of worship.

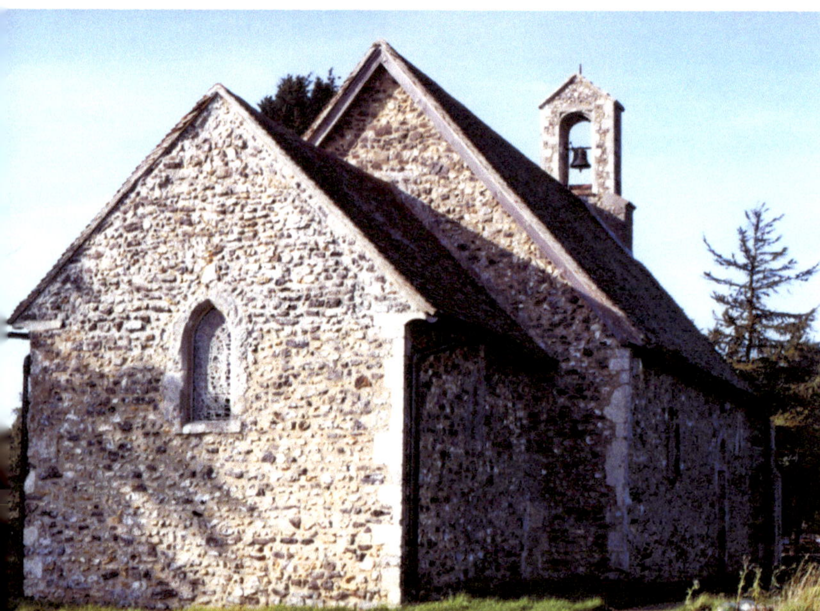

St Oswald's Church.

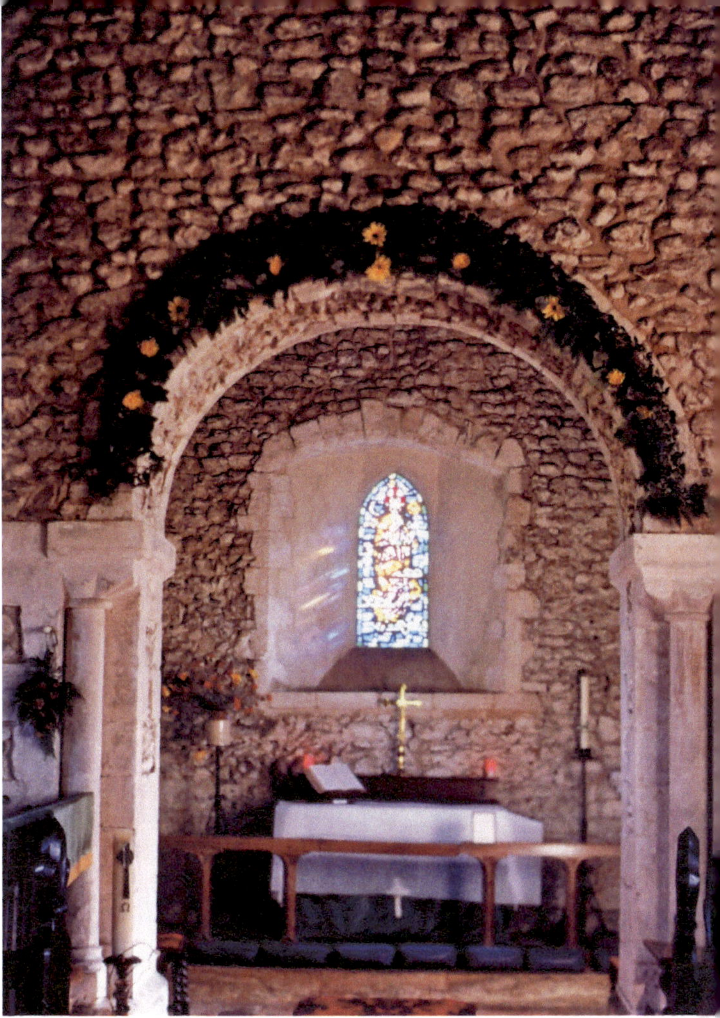

47. Elham Valley Way

A footpath 22.5 miles in length connects Hythe on the coast with Canterbury via the Elham Valley with its intermittent Nailbourne stream, string of interesting villages, woods and downland views. To do the whole thing might take eleven hours or more – most people, of course, do it in sections of their choice. I always think direction of travel is preferable, using Hythe as the starting point then you have the wonders of Canterbury with its plethora of refreshment venues at journeys end.

The first section passes through woods and downs along a green corridor, passing through Sene Wood and Seabrook Valley before reaching the start of the Elham Valley itself.

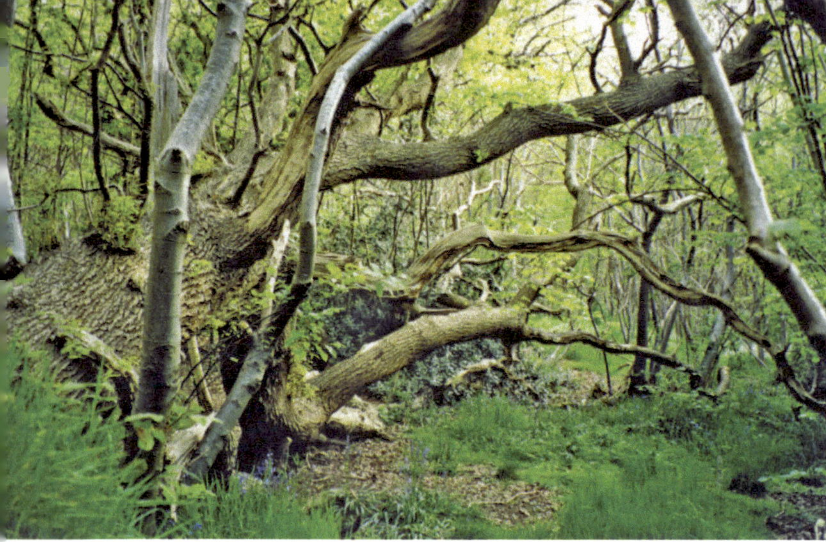

Sene Wood, north of Hythe.

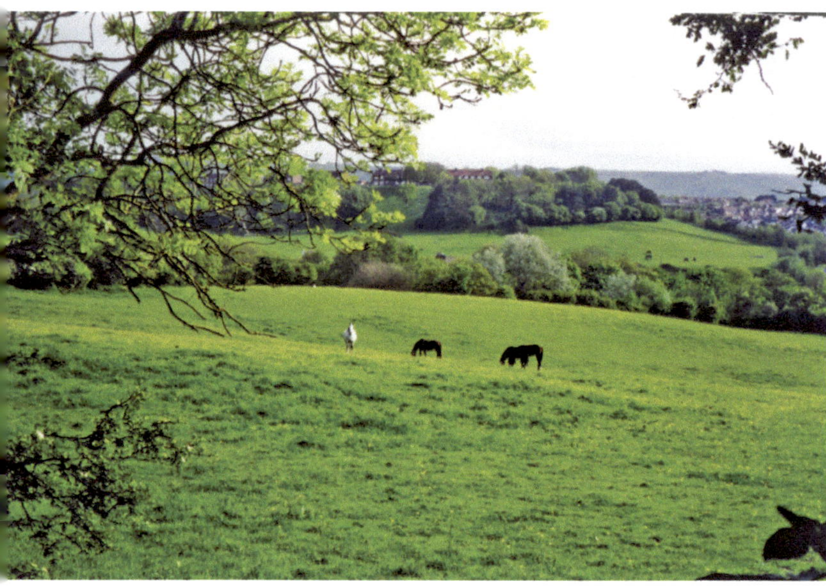

Seabrook Valley, near Hythe.

From the villages of Newington and Peene nestling beneath the smoothly scalloped escarpment of the Kent Downs the way follows roughly the old Elham Valley Railway Line, which finally closed in the 1950s, with some deviations and diversions here and there. A recreated station from the old line containing information on the history of the Elham Valley Railway and a restored steam engine can be found at the Peene Railway Museum.

A few miles north brings us to Lyminge, where the public library is housed in the village's old railway station. Lyminge was very important in the early Saxon period. The church of St Mary and St Ethelburga was founded in AD 633 along with a 'double house', a monastery/nunnery by Ethelburga the former Queen of Northumbria upon her return to Kent after the death of her husband King Edwin. Ethelburga was the first abbess and a stone marking the place where she was buried in AD 647 can be seen in the churchyard. Just down the hill

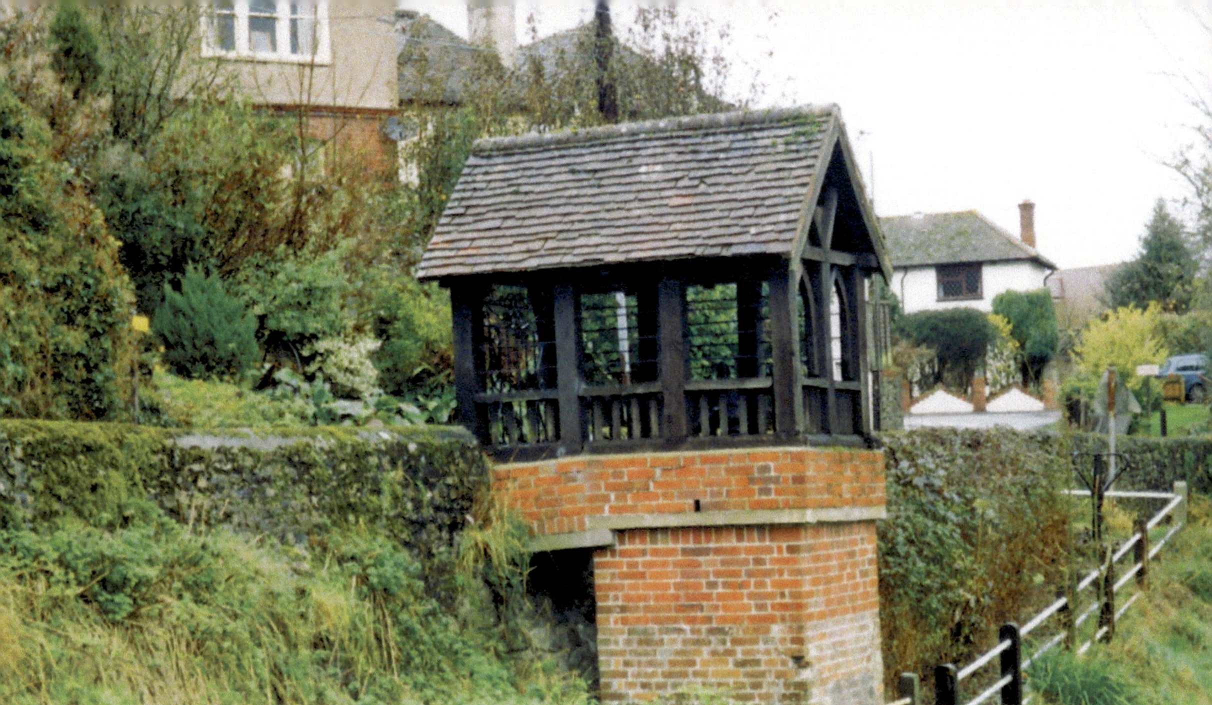

from the church is an interesting Victorian structure covering the wellhead of the Nailbourne stream, known as St Ethelburgas's Well. From here the stream flows north and appears and disappears according to the level of the water table. It passes Elham, where there are many attractive half-timbered houses; Barham, where it sometimes, in wet years, floods across the road; past Kingston with its pub, the Black Robin, named after a notorious highwayman; and on through tranquil cattle-grazed countryside past Bishopsbourne and Bridge. Further on the Nailbourne becomes less intermittent and known as the Little Stour at Patrixbourne as we have previously seen. Ultimately, the Little Stour and this long walk reaches Canterbury and hopefully a hostelry to welcome the weary traveller.

48. Lynsore Valley

Running parallel with the Elham Valley over the hills to the west, the Lynsore Valley is a hidden gem of unsung beauty along with the nearby countryside. From Barham a walk or cycle ride along the little lanes through Covet and Covert Woods take you through little hidden hollows and coombes, patches of forest and wood, coniferous and deciduous to arrive at a view of Lynsore Valley, a place on the map called Clambercrown.

At this junction a small cottage named Clambercrown tells you where you are and has an interesting story associated with it, fully told by author Jocelyn Brooke in an eloquent and humorous book entitled *The Dog at Clambercrown*. The 'dog' in question was a pub of that name, which the young Brooke had heard about as a child onwards, always mentioned as a rather inaccessible, mysterious place situated in remote countryside described as 'the back of beyond'. Over the years Brooke developed a fantasy of what this Dog at Clambercrown and its surrounding countryside were like. Eventually, at the age of sixteen, Brooke finally set out to find The Dog. The long, drawn-out expedition with all its adventures and setbacks make an interesting and entertaining read, and it is of great credit to the author that he fills a whole book satisfyingly mostly with details of this one relatively minor excursion. When Brooke finally reaches The Dog at Clambercrown it is a let-down; the pub has closed, he is offered a glass of milk by the former licensee and sets off home. The countryside turns out to be just the same as that he is used to, nothing strange or exotic as he had imagined, just the usual downs and trees to the horizon, on and on. Brooke comes to a rather depressing conclusion that 'life is futile' and decides this is his great, personal philosophical discovery. (It's a great read!)

The Lynsore Valley, looking towards Clambercrown.

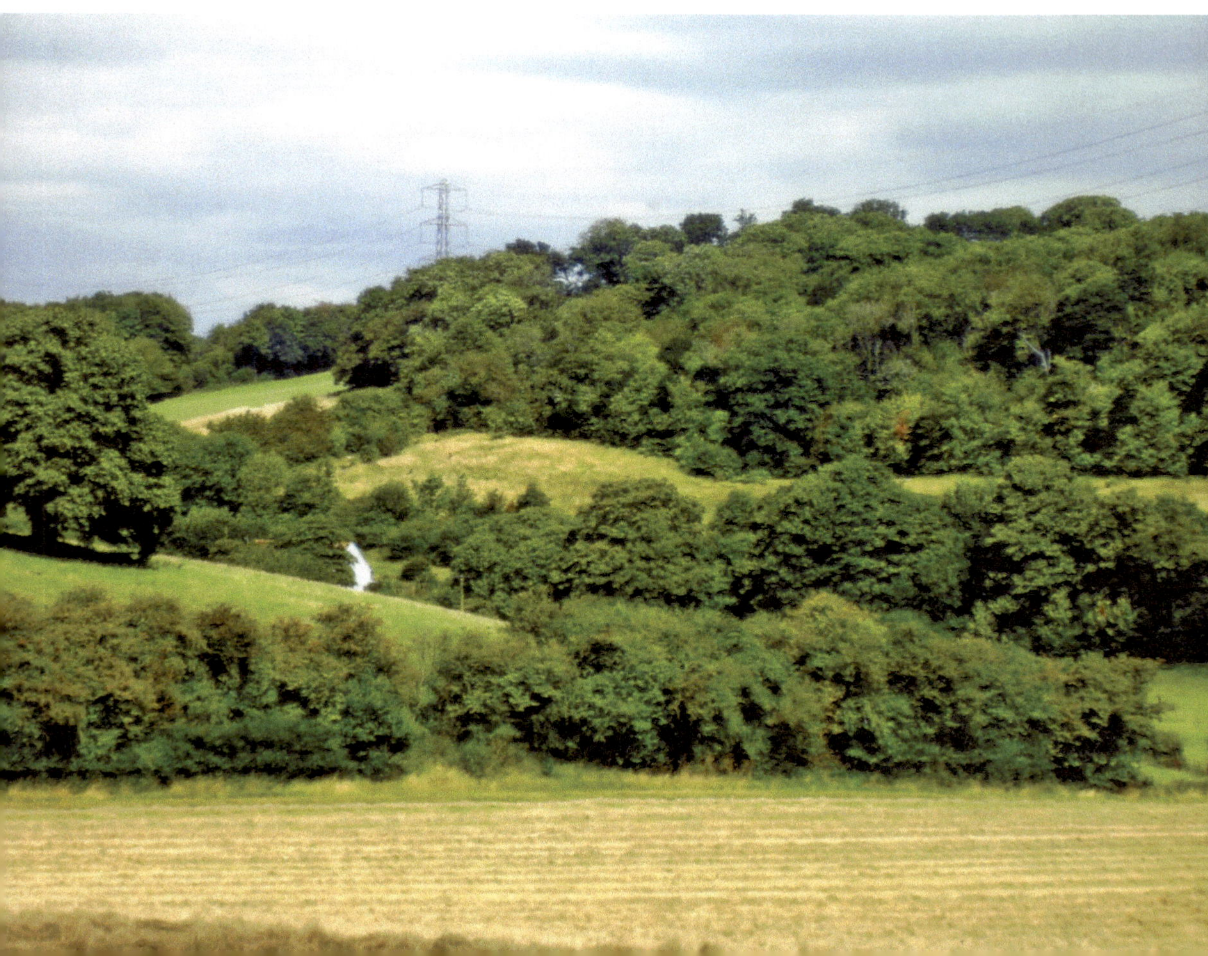

The countryside, of course, is not dull or monotonous but relaxing, unhurried, tranquil, a haven for wildlife and obviously a place for creative minds. Moving down from Clambercrown into the Lynsore Valley itself, the mixture of chalk grassland and ancient woodland is recognised by several wildlife organisations as important for a number of species, particularly orchids, grass snakes, adders and dormice. Buzzards wheel overhead along the woodland edges, pheasants squawk and run, naturalists furtively observe and take notes.

Down in the valley itself the hamlet of Pett Bottom was a favourite with author Ian Fleming, on account of The Duck Inn. A blue plaque on the wall tells how the novelist wrote one of his James Bond stories – *You Only Live Twice* – here in 1964. The Duck Inn features in the story as where the young James Bond was brought up by his great aunt.

Back up at Clambercrown, why not take a different route back to the public transport of the Elham Valley? Along narrow unfrequented lanes, past 'apple juice for sale' and a field full of huge pigs, to Marley, a hamlet that was once the home of sculptor Henry Moore. A blue plaque in a hedge celebrates Moore's former presence. From Marley it is a short distance to Kingston and perhaps to the Black Robin pub while waiting for a bus home.

Lynsore Valley from Quilters Wood.

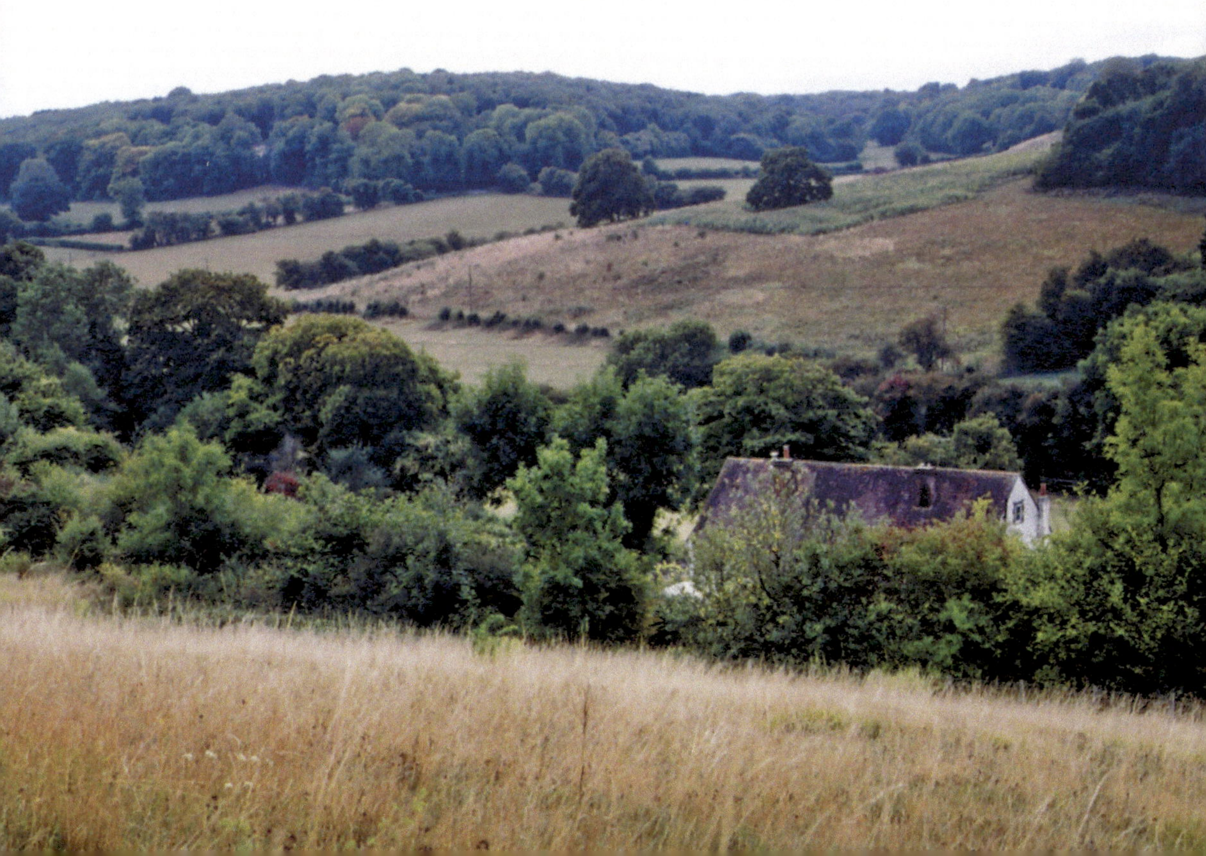

49. Chilham

This most picturesque of ancient East Kent villages lies about halfway between Canterbury and Ashford. It has a medieval square, which, along with the roads that lead to and from it, exhibit a stunning range of fifteenth- to sixteenth-century half-timbered houses. There is an annual May Day celebration held in the square of this quintessential old English village.

Not surprisingly Chilham has been well used in TV and films as a location. The classic 1944 film by Michael Powell and Emeric Pressburger titled *A Canterbury Tale* used Chilham as well as Chartham and Fordwich as the fictional village of 'Chillingbourne'. The village was also used as a location for Miss Marple and Poirot films and a TV adaptation of Jane Austen's *Emma*.

At either end of Chilham's village square are its church and its castle. The church is fifteenth century and is rumoured to have been the burial place of Thomas Becket. Chilham Castle was initially built in the twelfth century, though most of what you see now is Jacobean. The gardens laid out by John Tradescent and Capability Brown cover some 25 acres and include both formal gardens and historic parkland. These contain a heronry dating back to the thirteenth century and is said to be the oldest in the western world. There are between eighty to 100 heron nests per year, though I've never see so many of these birds in close proximity – where do they all go?

Chilham village square.

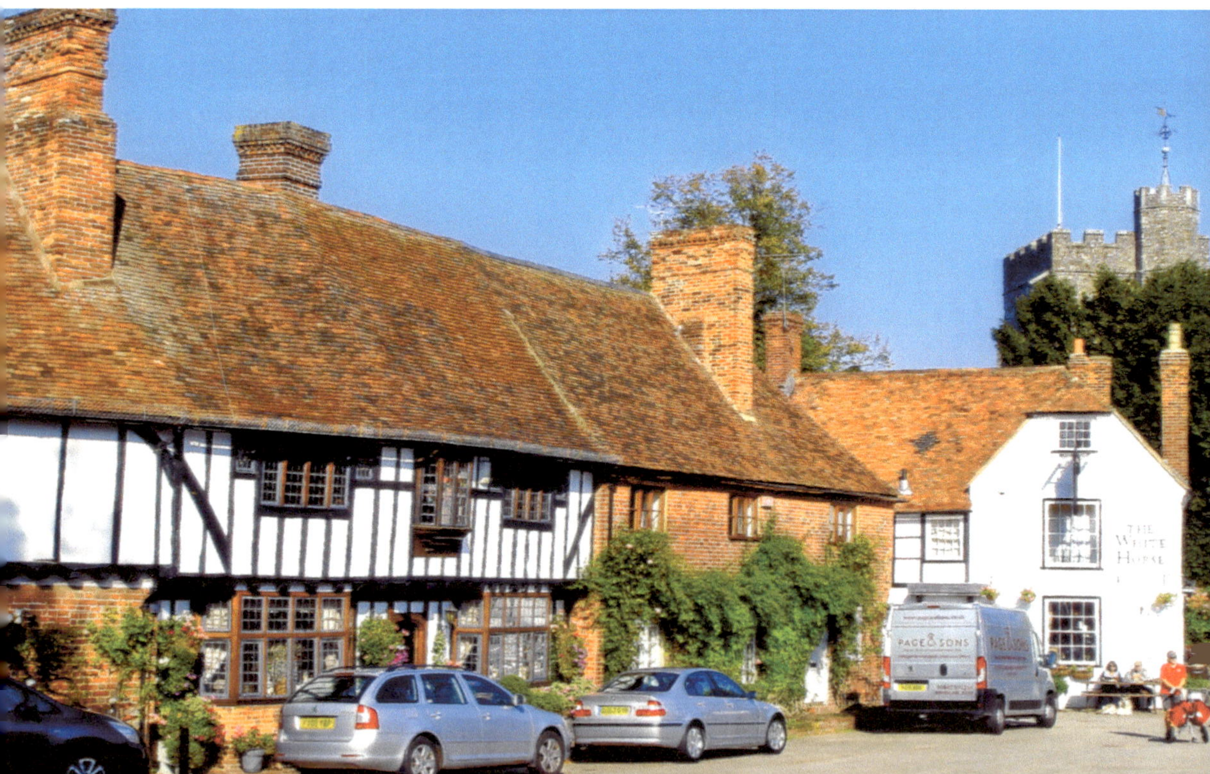

Chilham is one of these East Kent villages that has recently gained a beautiful wrought-iron village sign, which includes depictions of the church, old buildings, castle and heronry.

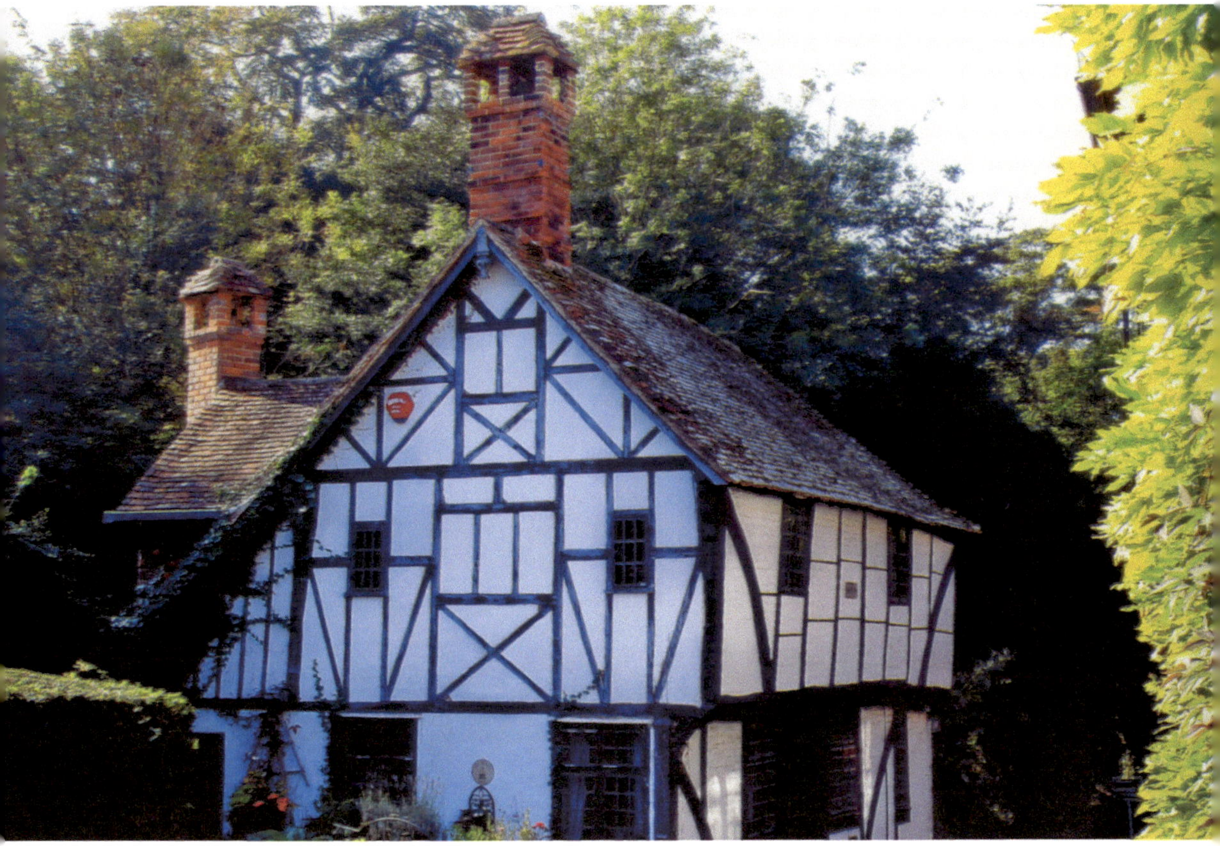

Above: Half-timbered house, Chilham.

Right: Chilham village sign.

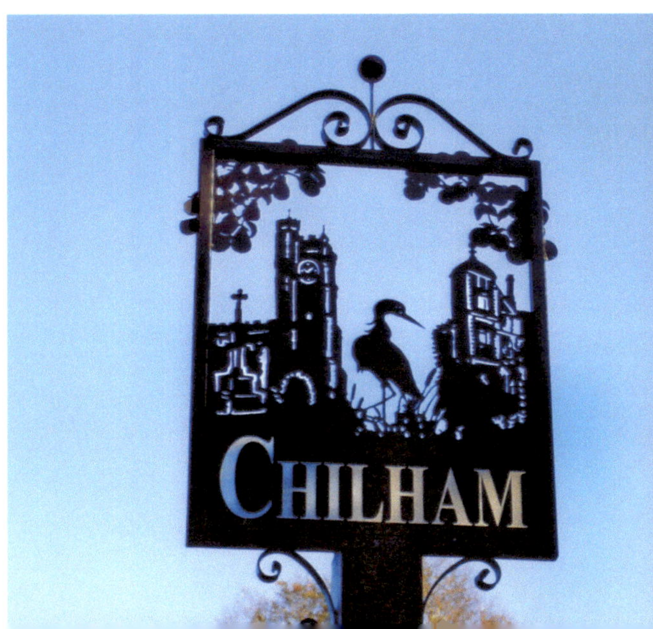

50. Kent Downs

The Kent Downs cover some 23 per cent of the land area of Kent, much of it an Area of Outstanding Natural Beauty (AONB). In these pages we have already covered many features and places within the Kent Downs, but the escarpment deserves special mention on account of its landscape quality. The Kent Downs escarpment from near Wye, just outside Ashford to the Folkestone Downs from where it eventually joins the sea to become the White Cliffs of Dover, are a particularly fine range of hills.

Above, the ancient town of Wye, the Devils Kneading Trough at around 550 feet above sea level, is a notably scenic spot with its smooth folds and coombe as well as having an expansive view across the Weald of Kent and towards distant Romney Marsh. Further east at the start of the Elham Valley between Etchinghill and Newington are similarly a striking series of spurs, folds and coombes whose smooth curves are particularly enhanced by the winter or evening sunshine.

The Kent Downs are an important wildlife habitat. The area around the Devils Kneading Trough known as the Wye and Crundale Downs is a National Nature Reserve on account of the quality of its chalk grassland, which has been grazed for centuries. This is recognised as the most flower-rich grassland in Kent, and with flowers come bees and butterflies. The latter are well represented by the blue butterflies, the common, chalkhill and, my favourite, the Adonis blue. A series of springs rise from the bases of the hills, pure, clean, hard, iron-rich spring water, purified by years of filtering through the chalk. As such they have formed the nucleus of ancient settlements or been revered as holy wells such as the Bronze Age village discovered between Sugar Loaf Hill and Round Hill at Folkestone, in an area known traditionally as Holywell.

Chalk hills from the earliest times have encouraged the creation of hill figures. Ancient carvings such as the Uffington White Horse in Berkshire or Cerne Abbas Giant in Dorset are well known. There may well have once been such figures in Kent, now long grassed over, but in more recent times any dearth of such images has been made up. In 1902 the Wye Crown was carved to commemorate the coronation of Edward VII. More recently, in 2003, the Folkestone White Horse was created by local artist Charles Newington in the Folkestone Downs behind the Channel Tunnel Terminal. Newington's white horse is an animated and alive image inspired by that on the downs at Uffington.

You can visit and explore the Kent Downs at certain points but to my mind to appreciate them fully, walk along the crest, enjoy the views, the updraught, the flowers, butterflies, magnificent skyscapes, the skylarks and the sunshine.

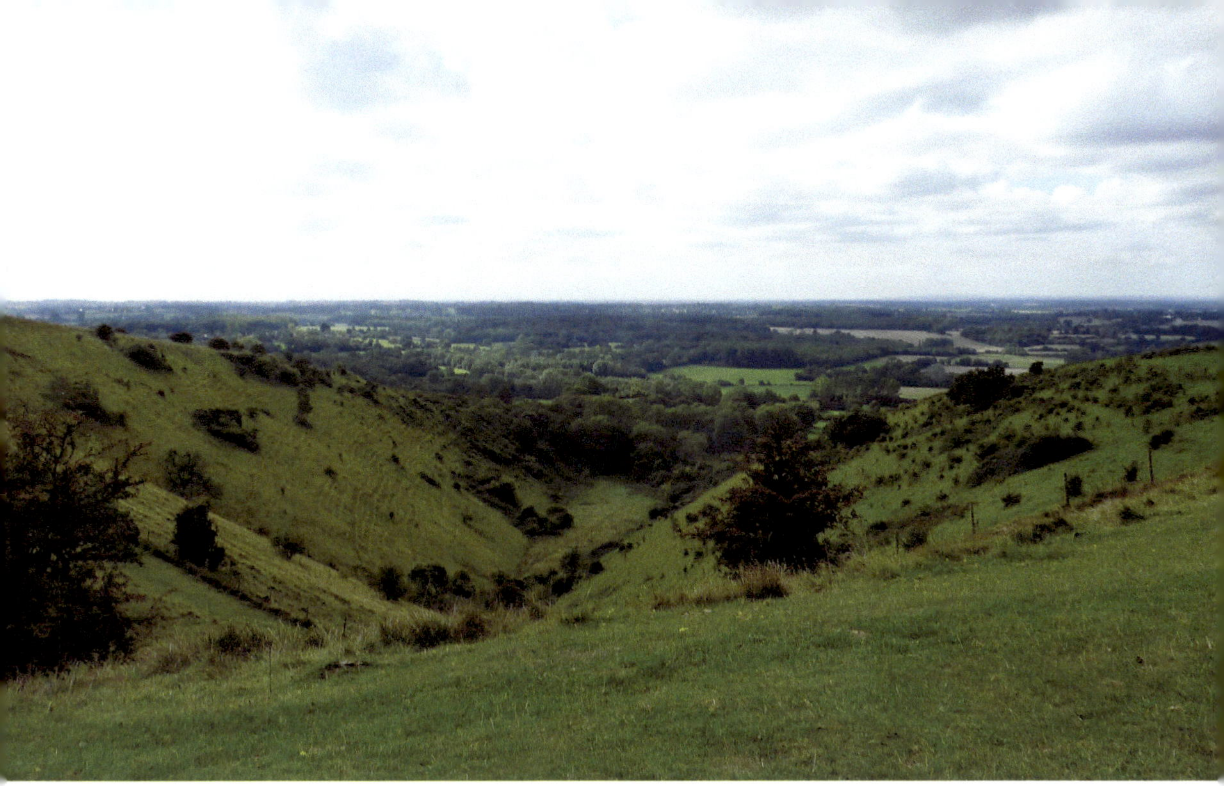

Above: Devil's Kneading Trough near Wye. (Photo by Steve Boulding)

Below: East Kent Downs. (Etching by Candida Wright)

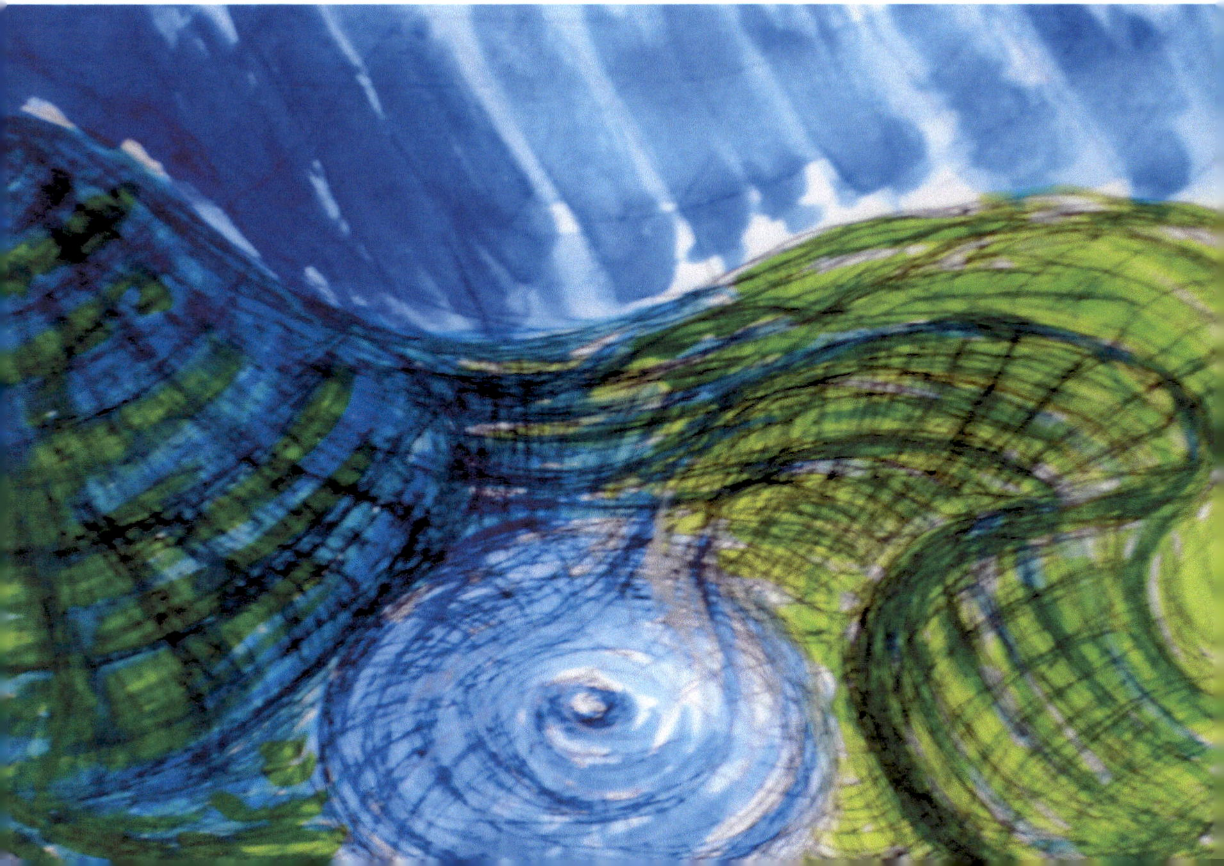

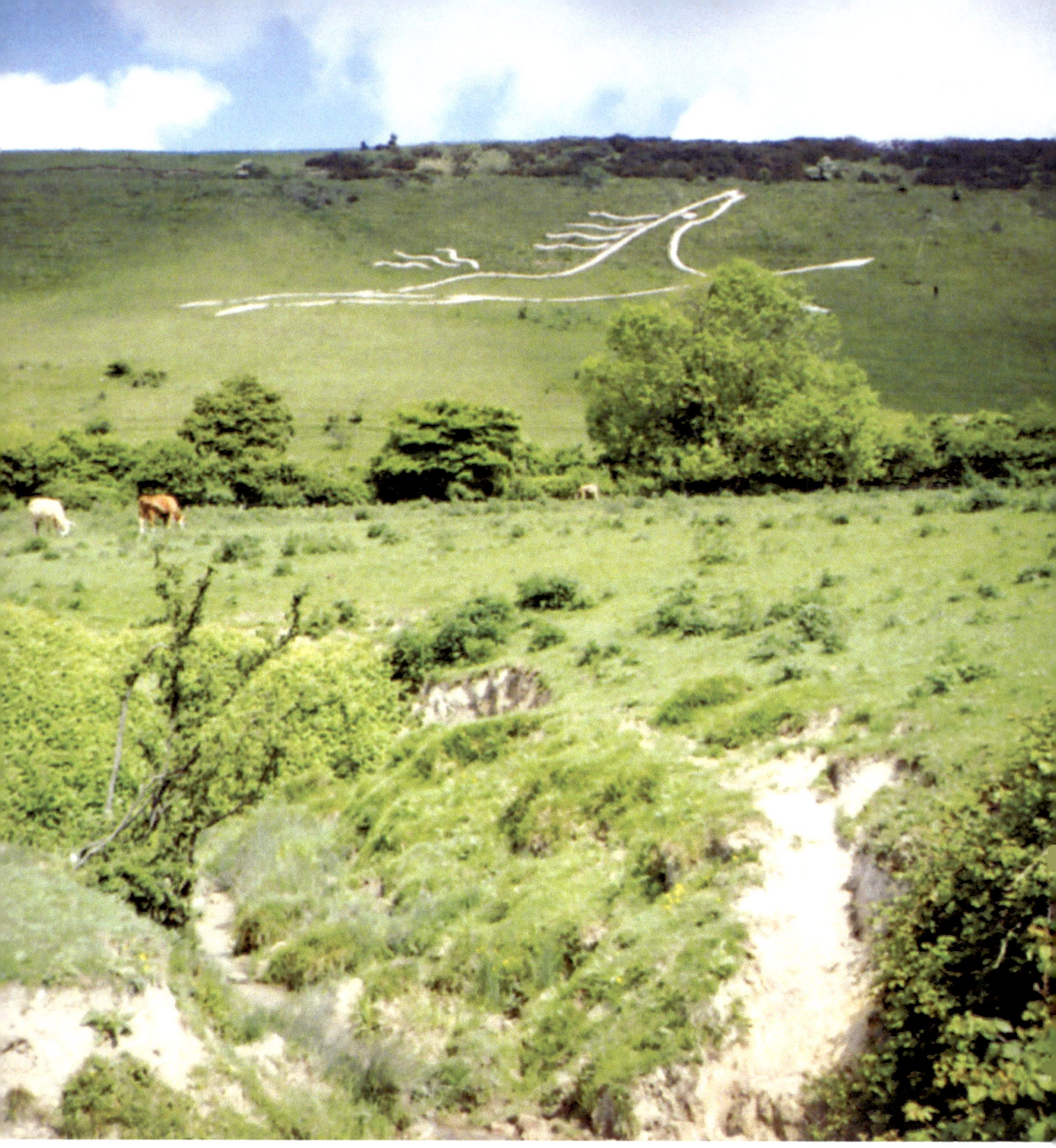

Folkestone White Horse.

Bibliography

Barham, Richard Harris, *The Ingoldsby Legends* (George Routledge and Sons, 1905)

Brooke, Jocelyn, *The Dog at Clambercrown – an Excursion* (Bodley Head, 1955)

Cook, Sam and Saunders, Claire, *The Rough Guide to Kent, Sussex and Surrey* (Rough Guides Ltd, 2017)

Fleming, Ian, *Moonraker* (Pan, 1955)

Guy, Sarah, *London on Sea – 50 Capital Days Out on the Coast* (Ebury Press 2018)

Harris, Paul. *The White Cliffs of Dover* (Amberley, 2013)

Hart, Brian, *Along and Around the Elham Valley Way* (Kent County Council, 1994)

Hollands, Ray and Harris, Paul, *Along the Kent Coast* (Sutton, 2003)

Kent Wildlife Trust, *Romney Marsh – A Brief Guide* (2008)

Roper, Anne, *The Gift of the Sea – Romney Marsh* (Birlings Ltd, 1984)

Smith, Nick Mayhew, *Britain's Holiest Places* (Lifestyle Press Ltd, 2011)

Tuson, Dan, *The Kent Downs* (The History Press, 2010)

Wilmott, Tony, *Richborough and Reculver* (English Heritage, 2016)

About the Author

Paul Harris was born in Tunbridge Wells and has also lived in Canterbury, Deal, Romney Marsh and Folkestone, so is a true 'man of Kent'.

He has worked in a number of tourism- and heritage-related roles in the county and has had over twenty local interest books published over the years.

Paul lives with his partner, artist/sculptor Candida Wright, in Folkestone's Creative Quarter and when not writing enjoys walking the local coast and countryside.

Other books by this author published by Amberley include:

The White Cliffs of Dover
The Jurassic Coast
Folkestone in 50 Buildings